IN BROOKE ASTOR'S COURT

An Insider's Story

BY ALICE MACYCOVE PERDUE
WITH JAMES W. SEYMORE

ISBN: 1500225029
ISBN 13: 9781500225025
Library of Congress Control Number: 2014912122
CreateSpace Independent Publishing Platform
North Charleston, South Carolina

IN MEMORIAM

AUTHOR'S NOTE

I was hired in November 1993 to work for Brooke Astor in her business office, paying her bills, managing the office, and serving as the assistant to her son, Anthony Marshall. For the first nine years, I very much enjoyed my job and all the people with whom I worked.

Then Mrs. Astor broke her hip in June 2003. As her health declined, and Mrs. Astor became increasingly isolated, I observed, almost daily, disturbing changes to the usual practices in the Astor office. I kept notes about anything that didn't seem appropriate to me and of my feelings and reactions to what I witnessed. I was dismissed by Mr. Marshall in September 2005. Most of the staff who had remained loyal to Mrs. Astor also were fired.

After the story of Brooke Astor's unseemly situation broke in July 2006, I listened to what was said in the news and read articles and commentary about the family relationships--and about elder abuse. I testified at Anthony Marshall's trial in 2009 when he was charged with stealing from his mother. On many occasions, I was approached by the media to speak out but never felt it was the right time to do so. Now is the right time.

I have written this book to set the record straight on what happened inside the Astor office and to Brooke Astor herself, a wonderful, charming, witty woman whom I greatly admired.

CHAPTER ONE

THE THUNDERBOLT

———⟨∞⟩———

I am not an early riser. So when my telephone rang at 7:30 a.m. on July 26, 2006, I was awakened from a deep sleep. A friend of mine was screaming into the phone, "Mrs. Astor is on the front page of the *Daily News*." That certainly got my attention, so I hung up, jumped into some clothes and ran out to buy a paper. As I approached the newsstand, I couldn't miss the red ink and the headline, DISASTER FOR MRS. ASTOR. Oh dear, someone had spilled the beans.

The news hit New York like a thunderbolt. The legendary philanthropist Brooke Astor, heiress to one of America's fabled fortunes, the doyenne of New York society for scores of years, the woman who had given hundreds of millions to hundreds of charities, was alleged to be living in squalor.

Crippled by a broken hip and enfeebled by age at 104, she was said to be sleeping on a urine-stained sofa in her Park Avenue duplex, shut off from her friends and abandoned to a lonely, twilight life. It would have been sad to learn of any elderly woman suffering in such fashion, but Brooke Astor! The woman who *defined* style and charity and wealth and civic virtue? Her pathetic condition was rapidly becoming the greatest society scandal in recent memory.

The spark that lit up this shocking story was a court petition filed by Philip Marshall, Brooke Astor's concerned grandson and a professor of historic preservation at Roger Williams University in Bristol, Rhode Island. Philip was asking the court to remove his 82-year-old father, Anthony D. Marshall, as Mrs. Astor's guardian and replace him with Mrs. Astor's dear friend, Annette de la Renta, and JP Morgan Chase. Anthony was Mrs. Astor's only son and had her power of attorney. Philip alleged in his petition that his father had thrown his grandmother into this misery while conniving to steal her fortune. The *New York Times* covered the story for months, the tabloids had a field day, gossip columns nation-wide fed on the allegations, and magazines jockeyed for information by taking sides with one part of the family or the other. Like a Greek tragedy of son against mother and father against son, the scandal fed on itself, ultimately resulting in Anthony Marshall's criminal conviction.

Meanwhile, as all New York chewed over the tawdry details of this last, tragic chapter of Brooke Astor's life, I was one of the few who had witnessed the story behind the story. I had worked in Mrs. Astor's business office for 12 years, and my boss was Anthony Marshall himself. I saw at first hand what was happening behind the scenes of Mrs. Astor's public life, and I knew the facts. And then, as preparation for the court hearing began, I became increasingly drawn into the ugly story. I was called into meetings with lawyers, investigators, bankers, even forensic accountants, to tell them what I knew. I saw jaws drop when these professionals heard my tales. But this one sad chapter is not the whole story of Brooke Astor's life, and the piteous image she presented at the end is not how she should be remembered. What is important to re-member about Brooke Astor is the good she did for others and the wonderful way she lived her life.

I wrote this book to record what I knew of her and what happened to her, as I saw it, and as I lived it, and with as much detail as I can muster. I owe it to her to set the record straight.

So let me tell you how this scandal began...

CHAPTER TWO

IN THE BEGINNING

—✸✸✸—

It was a cold and typically gloomy New York evening in January 2006. I was curled up with a book in my Manhattan apartment when the phone rang.

"Alice? This is Philip Marshall. Happy New Year."

"Philip! How good to hear from you. Happy New Year to you, too!" I had met Philip Marshall only once, at a book party thrown by Mrs. Astor at the Central Park Zoo in honor of the publication of his father's book *Zoo* in May of 1994. But I had talked to Philip many times by phone and I liked his friendly and unassuming manner. Philip, a tall slender man in his 50s who practiced Buddhism, was married and had two children. He lived in Massachusetts. At that point, however, I had no idea what his relationship was with his father.

"I was just visiting my grandmother at Christmas," Philip continued, "and I found out you had been let go! When did that happen? Why?"

"Well, Philip, I was fired last September," I answered. "I think your father and stepmother let me go because I wasn't in their 'camp.' They've let several of Mrs. Astor's long-term, loyal employees go. Initially, I was shocked by my dismissal but then I realized that I was actually relieved. Things just had not been right in the office for quite some time."

"I want to talk to you about that... and about my grandmother," Philip said. "Based on what I've heard from her staff, I understand you have some things to tell me."

Indeed I did. It was a sad story, but one that needed telling. So as evening fell that January night, I settled down for a long chat with Philip about the darkness that had crept over his grandmother's life for the past several years.

Philip knew that even into her 101st year, his grandmother Brooke had remained curious about the world and helpful to lots of people in it. He knew that I had worked for her for more than a decade, reporting to Anthony, Philip's father, who handled her personal investments and business affairs.

For a dozen years, from 1993 to 2005, it had been exciting for me to be a small part of the inner workings of a fascinating world that most people rarely encounter.

It was a world of luxurious homes, great art, fabulous jewels, the most gorgeous gowns, and glittering evenings among the rich and powerful. During those years Mrs. Astor gave away tens of millions of dollars, a small portion of the hundreds of millions she had given away over her lifetime. She was revered in New York City for her extraordinary generosity, her style, her civic-mindedness—and even for her longevity.

I don't mean to make her sound saintly or sticky-sweet. She was sharp. She was strong-willed, and she had strong opinions. Her displeasure could cut like a whip, but she was also the soul of generosity, both publicly and privately. Though she had outlived most of her friends, she showed almost no decline in her ebullience and energy. Simply put, she was fun. She enjoyed good company, good conversation, and good times. She thrived on stimulation and a busy, outgoing life. She was twice my age, but we gossiped together. We occasionally had lunch together. I adored her.

Philip knew all about her great qualities, but he didn't know what had been going on in his grandmother's recent life. For example, her favorite artwork--Childe Hassam's *Flags, Fifth Avenue*--had been sold. Shortly after her 101st birthday, Brooke Astor fell and broke her hip for the second time—after which things began to change rapidly. Her health declined. Anthony and his third wife, Charlene, became more... *active* in Mrs. Astor's finances.

I told Philip that after her accident—when she could no longer stand up for herself physically and mentally—Mrs. Astor's will had been changed. Large sums had been transferred from Mrs. Astor to the Marshalls. Then the respected, old-line law firm, Sullivan & Cromwell, which she had retained for decades, had suddenly been dismissed, replaced by a friend of the Marshalls, Francis X. Morrissey, Jr., an attorney who had been suspended from practicing law in New York State for two years back in the 1990s and who appeared to have a hand in every new movement of Mrs. Astor's money. Old friends were being denied permission to visit Mrs. Astor, and she had become increasingly shut off from the world. Even the bounty of flowers that used to surround her had disappeared. The list of deprivations went on and on.

Philip sounded agitated by what I told him, but for me it was a great relief to unburden myself. I had kept it all inside. For the final two-and-one-half years before I was fired in 2005, I had seen what was happening, but I hadn't known what to do about it. For years I had been in the middle between mother and son, and they were so different in character. Mr. Marshall was always "thrifty" and totally self-absorbed. Where Mrs. Astor was generous, he was stingy. Where she was gregarious, Mr. Marshall was introverted. Where she delighted in fun, he could be dour and suspicious. Physically, Mrs. Astor was petite, always dressed and made up beautifully, and "electric." Mr. Marshall was a nice-looking man, but his manner was languid.

So on that winter evening I told Philip everything, even though I knew it was painful for him to hear what I was saying. I know he talked to others after our phone conversation and investigated further. He enlisted the support of his grandmother's close friends, David Rockefeller and Annette de la Renta. Then Philip filed a court petition, accusing his father of neglecting Mrs. Astor and diverting her money for his own use. The petition was supposed to remain private, but someone—I think someone in the courthouse—leaked the news, and the scandal broke.

But now I'll back up and tell you a little bit about myself. I've lived in Manhattan my entire adult life, though I'm told I still have my Boston accent. I still *pahk tha cah in Havahd yahd*. Born and reared in Boston and Newton, Massachusetts, I graduated from the University of Massachusetts in Amherst and moved to Manhattan right after college, and I've been here ever since. I met and married my husband, Joe, here. In fact, I've lived in the same apartment on the East Side of Manhattan for over 40 years—I hate to admit it, but it's true. How boring!

I worked in the magazine business most of my career, usually in sales promotion, but in 1993 I was out of work. I took on several freelance projects--one of them was an advertising section on Hawaii for *Travel & Leisure*--but they didn't take much time. So I thought, *Gee, why not fill some time with temporary work?* and I registered with a temp agency recommended by a friend.

I'd go to the agency a couple of times a week to work on a computer tutorial, and one time I was sitting there and a staffer poked her head in the doorway and said, "Do you know who Brooke Astor is?" And I said, "Well, sure." And she said, "Would you be interested in a *permanent* position?" And I thought, *Not really*--but I asked what it was about. She said, "It's mainly paying her bills." That didn't seem like something I'd want to do for long, but I decided it wouldn't hurt to go for an interview. So one was set up for me with Mrs. Astor's son, Anthony Marshall, in his office on Park Avenue.

The office was small, consisting of three rooms on the 17th floor of a building at Park Avenue and 54th Street. It was conservatively furnished, and quite utilitarian--nothing fancy. On the walls of Mr. Marshall's office were many photographs taken of his travels, especially his travels in Africa; he had been Ambassador to Kenya back in the 1970s. He had a very upper-crust accent, and his manner was formal. But we had a lovely chat and he told me what the job entailed.

The next night I was out having dinner with my sister Susan and our erudite cousin Lewis--we always called him Luxy (look-see)--at B. Smith's in the theatre district, a restaurant known for its southern style cooking, and we were chatting about our family. At one point I went to the ladies' room. When I got back, the first thing Luxy said to me was, "Did you know that Brooke Astor was born in Portsmouth, New Hampshire?" I looked at my sister. "You told him about my interview, didn't you," I said. And she said, "No, I didn't." They had been talking about Portsmouth because my mother and her siblings grew up there. And I told Luxy, "Well, that's strange! I just had an interview with her son for a job working in her business office!" And we thought this was quite a coincidence.

That's the first sign I had that all this was meant to be—that I was destined to work for Mrs. Astor, to see everything that happened to her over the next decade, and to write this book that you're reading now. Just then, the maitre d' passed by our table calling out, "There is a phone call for Alice Perdue." (This was life before the ubiquitous cell phone.) My husband had tracked me down to say Mr. Marshall had phoned and wanted me to come to his office for a second interview. I asked my husband to please call him back and set up the meeting since I was in a noisy restaurant.

So the next day I went to talk with Mr. Marshall again, and this time he brought in his wife, Charlene. She was about my age, in her mid-forties (more than two decades younger than her husband), blonde, wearing a cotton turtleneck and cardigan sweater. She looked very unsophisticated. She was friendly, open, and seemed unpretentious.

Mr. Marshall asked me why I would want this position. I told him straight out that it seemed like a normal job where I could come in, do my work, go home, and not take it with me. I had lived and breathed my job —working on a travel magazine. I'd work late and then take my work home, and I hated that. It was all consuming, and I was always complaining. At this job, I could walk to work, I'd get a decent salary, four weeks' vacation, and health-insurance coverage for both my husband and me. And the Marshalls seemed to be very nice. The work, though it wouldn't be creative, would keep me busy, and I liked that. It sounded interesting to me— because it was for Mrs. Astor. That evening, Mr. Marshall called again and offered me the job. I took it.

I started as a temporary, and I was offered a permanent position two weeks later. (I found out that the woman I was replacing was dying of cancer and had been out for six months. They had held the job open for her--that's how nice they were then. It was sad, but she finally passed away.)

It was a small office--just Mr. Marshall, who handled his mother's personal investments; Lourdes Hilario, a Filipina with a pleasant smile and a nice personality (and an MBA), who handled the bookkeeping, payroll, and banking and assisted with investments; and me, the person who paid the bills and functioned as the office manager. I was also the executive assistant to Mr. Marshall.

We had those three rooms on the top floor at Park Avenue and 54th Street, which I came to love as my aerie in the sky. A door connected us to the much larger offices of the Vincent Astor Foundation where additional people worked. The foundation, which had been established in 1948, was known for giving grants to institutions in New York City only, because that was where the Astors had made their fortune. Mrs. Astor had her office there—a big, beautiful corner office—and Linda Gillies, who was the very capable and attractive director of the foundation, had her office there too. Linda was a font of information, and I could always go to her for good counsel. There were a number of other rooms. One of them was a large walk-in safe that Vincent Astor had had constructed when the office building was new. Important foundation documents were kept there.

One of the first things I had to do was to familiarize myself with the place by reading the files, most of which were kept behind my desk. They were just fascinating. For instance, I'd be reading about Mrs. Astor's charitable donations, and I'd come across a handwritten thank-you note from Nelson Rockefeller. Or I'd find all Mrs. Astor's old passports with stampings from all over the world; or contracts for yachts she had chartered in Europe; or records about the cars she had owned—there were tons of those—or records of her apartments in New York and her estate in Westchester, Holly Hill, where she spent every weekend, or of Cove End, her summer home up in Northeast Harbor, Maine. Or I'd come across records of the different dogs she had owned, or purchases of jewelry, antiques, furniture—whatever.

That's where I first saw the file of her purchase of Childe Hassam's famous painting *Flags, Fifth Avenue*, which she loved so much she'd hung it prominently in her apartment, right over the fireplace in her red-lacquered library. Yes, that's the painting Mr. Marshall sold in 2002 and that later became so important in the family's nasty legal battle. (More about that later). I was a little surprised that right away I had access to so much personal information; that made me wonder about how trusting Mr. Marshall was. I assumed he did a good background check on me!

From the start, Mr. Marshall asked me to call him just that— "Mr. Marshall." He asked me what I wanted to be called. "Alice," I said. It became somewhat awkward to call his wife "Charlene" if her husband was "Mr." to me, so I started calling her "Mrs. Marshall," although that always sounded so stilted to me, because we were contemporaries.

The first time I met Mrs. Astor, I thought she was sleeping. It was at the office Christmas luncheon in 1993. I had been working there only a couple of weeks, and I didn't know what to expect when they told me the party would be held in Mrs. Astor's private office. I wasn't nervous, but I was really *curious*. I wanted to meet her. Everyone in New York knew who Brooke Astor was. Her picture was in the society columns every week. She was a legend. And now I was going to meet her face-to-face. It was exciting!

So, at the appointed time, I stepped into her big corner office facing south and west on Park Avenue for the Christmas luncheon. The pale cream walls bore a large portrait of her deceased husband, Vincent Astor, in his Navy Captain's uniform; a collection of crystal apples on a table signified that Mrs. Astor was the "fairy godmother of the Big Apple;" and the furniture, I had been told, came from Vincent's yacht, the *Nourmahal*. I found my chair with several little gifts on it. It was the custom for staff members to give token presents to one another (I remember I bought chocolate Santas for everyone that year) so that we would have lots of little gifts to open. I picked up my gifts, sat down, and looked around the room.

It was a small intimate group: just the three who worked for the Astor Foundation; a few older people—I remember one gentleman from India who had worked for the foundation years ago; Mrs. Astor and her social secretary, Lorene Latine; and the three of us from the business office. Mrs. Astor was wearing a beautiful suit and a big hat and was sitting at her large partner's desk with her head down. I couldn't see her face because of her hat, and I thought, *Well, maybe she likes to take little naps.*

Nobody said anything for several minutes, and I thought, *Oh, that's very nice. They let her take a nap because she's 91, an elderly lady, and if she wants to doze off for a few minutes, that's okay, and...* Then she looked up, and her eyes were just sparkling and lively. I could see that Mr. Marshall had given her something to sign, and she had been reading it. She hadn't been napping at all. In fact—as I was to find out—she was a dynamo. She was *electric.* That's the best way I can describe her. She was up and about, here and there—she never sat still. She would come into the office and just exhaust everyone around her and keep going. Some little old lady!

Anyway, it was a very pleasant, cozy afternoon at the Christmas party. It lasted only an hour or two. They poured some champagne, we all opened our presents and chatted, and Mrs. Astor insisted on serving us herself. Linda Gillies, who always made the arrangements for the party, had had little tea sandwiches sent up from William Poll on Lexington Avenue—they were *delicious*—and also yummy little desserts. Mrs. Astor got up and passed the tray herself. She very much wanted to be the hostess, and she was so nice to everyone.

We all got a Christmas check as well as little gifts. Mrs. Astor gave me an autographed copy of *Patchwork Child*, her memoir of her childhood, which had just been reissued, and Mr. Marshall gave me a beautiful picture frame from the Metropolitan Museum of Art. I was so pleased--I had only been there a couple of weeks, and I really wasn't expecting anything. This was such a lovely beginning. I knew right then that I was going to love this job, and I did love it for many years. We had those little Christmas parties until the Astor Foundation closed to the public at the end of 1997. After that, Mr. Marshall did nothing for us around the holidays...but that's another story.

Left to right: Lourdes Hilario, Anthony Marshall,
Alice Perdue with Mrs. Astor

Left to right: Jackie Farrell, John Konrath,
Linda Gillies with Mrs. Astor

It was a very happy office during my early years there. Lourdes and I got along famously. We became like sisters because we spent so much time together. Lourdes, who was born in the Philippines, is honest beyond honest. I mean, I couldn't get the lady to fib if her life depended on it. She's very naïve and very straightforward, which sometimes could be really comical. She says what she's thinking. It goes right from her mind to her mouth with no editing, which occasionally caused her some problems. She's a couple of years older than me, but has a young-looking face framed by short, dark hair. She's a lovely woman, and I hope we always remain close.

For many years, Mr. Marshall was very good to me. On a couple of occasions, he gave me his tickets to a dress rehearsal at the Metropolitan Opera and let me go for the rest of the day to enjoy the opera at Lincoln Center. I took my sister and we had a grand time. I recall that we saw *I Puritani* and *Lucia di Lamamoor.*

He was always the gentleman and he seemed to appreciate my organizational skills and dedication. I paid 300 or so bills every month, and I did a lot of investigating of, and interacting with, the suppliers. One time I opened Mrs. Astor's American Express bill and saw several charges for purchases at Kmart totaling close to $4,000. I was immediately suspicious because I'd never known her to shop there. After checking with her driver and a couple of maids, I determined that these were not her purchases, so I spent quite a while negotiating with American Express. I was also responsible for the staff's health-insurance policy as the group administrator. Mrs. Astor had 23 employees then. Most were domestics— maids and butlers and gardeners and so forth—and I had to handle the insurance for all of them. Have you ever had to deal with insurance companies? *Ach,* a nightmare. But I did it. Over the years, I kept thinking that I should be getting combat pay for my tenacity in dealing with the stubborn insurance company. Sometimes I would have to steel myself for a three-hour phone call that would test my sanity. "Press one," "press two"—and then a disconnect. *Grrrr.*

Mrs. Astor used to send her chauffeur every so often to the office to pick up $500 cash, which was her tip money. One day, early in my employment, I was the only one in the office when her maid called and said that Mrs. Astor needed $500 and the car would be by shortly to pick it up. Lourdes normally took care of this, and I had no idea where she got the cash. So I ran out to my own bank across the street and took out $500 and *lent* it to Mrs. Astor!!! Little old me lending Mrs. Astor money—what a hoot!

But the first week I was there, something strange did happen. I was getting ready to send out the checks and the mail, and Mr. Marshall, who came in an hour or two each day, noticed one of them. He said, "I'm going to visit him later today. Take off the stamp, and I'll hand-deliver it." So I thought, *Well, okay, he's trying to send me a message: Just because we work in Mrs. Astor's office doesn't mean that we can waste money.* So I did it. I didn't have time to steam off the stamp, so I peeled it off with my fingernail and gave him the letter, and he left. (The stamp was so chewed up that I had to throw it away anyway.)

Then, a few days later, I was opening the mail, and a lot of it was junk I thought should be thrown out. One piece was the *Reader's Digest* sweepstakes. I was about to toss it when Lourdes saw me and said, "Oh, no, no, no! He likes those.

He sends those in." I said, "Oh, really?" I mean, when mine arrives in the mail I just throw it out. So I thought, *Hmmm. That's kind of peculiar. But I guess some people just like doing that kind of thing. Even the wealthy.* I had a feeling right from the start that Mr. Marshall was very thrifty, and as the years went by...well, in my estimation his thriftiness was so extreme that it was an illness.

Now, as I mentioned, Mrs. Astor was the exact opposite. She was Lady Bountiful—and interested in everything. Her life revolved around the Vincent Astor Foundation, of which she was the president, so she was always thinking about giving away money, and I don't mean just from the Astor Foundation. She gave away millions of her personal money to many organizations, and there were *hundreds* of them. She was generosity personified. Her biggies were the Metropolitan Museum of Art—she was a member of the Chairman's Council, which required dues of $40,000 when I first went to work in the office; a member of the Roundtable at the Morgan Library, which required dues of $20,000 a year; and a fellow of the Frick Collection, which was only $1,200.

But the New York Public Library was very special to her for several reasons. She had been an avid reader from a very young age, and the founding father, John Jacob Astor, had left $400,000 when he died in 1848 to establish a public library, which opened in 1849 (the original building is now the Public Theater down on Astor Place). So Mrs. Astor gave generously both through the Foundation and from her personal funds to the Library. She was one of the Literary Lions, and, for their gala dinner every year to raise money, would buy a table for $25,000, or $50,000.

Oh, there were so *many* organizations. There was Save Venice, Channel Thirteen, The Wildlife Conservation Society, the Animal Medical Center, as well as *several* literacy groups in the city. And charities up in Maine-- the Northeast Harbor Library, the College of the Atlantic, the Marine Biology Laboratory, and so on. The first year I was there she gave away almost $500,000 of her own money in addition to the millions the Astor Foundation granted.

Mrs. Astor also belonged to a lot of clubs—the Knickerbocker Club, the Colony Club, the Century Association—and for years the office was paying full dues to the Sleepy Hollow Country Club up in Westchester. Then we realized, Wait a minute!— this lady is over 90 years old. She doesn't play golf. So we cut that down to a social membership, since Mrs. Astor went to Sleepy Hollow only to walk her dogs on the golf course. But Mrs. Astor liked to support whatever establishments she felt contributed to her environment, whether she frequented them or not. In Maine, she belonged to everything—the beach and tennis club, the yacht club, and many others.

She was just generous by nature. She performed so many small acts of kindness that only the recipient ever knew about. For instance, there was an elderly lady friend of hers who must have been having financial troubles, and Mrs. Astor quietly paid her dues to the Knickerbocker Club for years and years. And to help out an elderly gentleman of her acquaintance (I think he was in ill health), Mrs. Astor made sure that a food basket from Marche Madison, a gourmet market on Madison Avenue, was sent to his apartment every week so he'd at least have some food in the house. These are just small things, but she repeated them many times over.

And here's an example personal to me: Soon after I began to work in the office, I got a call from Mrs. Astor asking me to help her update her address book. I went to her office, and we sat there for a while going through her book. (A funny thing: When we got to Doris Duke, the tobacco heiress, Mrs. Astor said, "Oh, you can take her out. She's dead." Then she leaned over to me conspiratorially and whispered, "You know, she left all her money to her *butler.*" *Quel scandale!*) When I completed the task, Mr. Marshall said to me, "My mother would like to give you something for helping her with her address book. Is there anything you need?" So I joked, "I could use a new wing on my little house on Cape Cod!" Mr. Marshall smiled. Then I said, "Well, I am in need of a new wallet." A few days later he presented me with a beautiful T. Anthony green leather wallet with my initials on it.

Mrs. Astor was always generous to her staff—sometimes in charming, wacky ways. One day, in 2001, I got a call from Mrs. Astor; she said, "I want you and Lourdes to go out and buy a pair of shoes." I was taken aback. So I said, "Mrs. Astor, that's very kind of you, but it's unnecessary." And she said, "No, no, no. I just want you to go out and buy some shoes." She had told everyone who worked in the apartment, at the office, at Holly Hill--everyone--to buy some shoes! Now some of us *really* got some nice shoes. One woman who worked at the apartment (she was very stylish and she could wear those very high heels) bought a pair of Manolo Blahniks. Lourdes and I went trotting over to Saks, and we found a shoe sale. We had fun trying on all sorts of shoes, and both ended up with Salvatore Ferragamos—but we paid maybe $150, tops. I thought it was the most charming gesture. It must have cost her several thousand dollars! Shoes! What made her think of that?

But Lourdes and I would worry about Mr. Marshall's reaction. I mean, Mrs. Astor would tell her chauffeur to go buy a warm winter coat because he was outside a lot. Or she'd tell her butler to get a new suit. And they'd do it and send us the bill. I'd write a check and give it to Mr. Marshall to sign, and he'd breathe a heavy sigh.

I dreaded this reaction of his so much that before I went shopping for the shoes I had never taken advantage of Mrs. Astor's offers. One day, for instance, she had gone to see a Broadway show—I think it was *Forever Tango* or *Tango Argentina*—and she thought it was just wonderful. She came into the office and told Lourdes and me to take our husbands and she'd pay for the tickets. Another time she told me to take my husband to see the famous pianist and singer Bobby Short play at the Carlyle Hotel because she *loved* that. But we didn't do either. We were too concerned about Mr. Marshall's likely reaction. But when the shoe thing came up, I decided to stick to my guns. When he called the office I told him, "Mr. Marshall, I just want you to know that Mrs. Astor told us all to buy shoes." And he sighed and said "There she goes again." I responded by saying I thought it was such a charming gesture, whereupon he said, "Do what you want." That was not a vote of approval!

Despite Mrs. Astor's generosity, there were inconsistencies in how employees were compensated. I'm not sure exactly who was responsible for these inconsistencies, but they always struck me as unfair. Some of us got bonuses, some did not. Often, it was simply that the squeaky wheel got the oil.

For instance, Mrs. Astor's custom was to give some of her staff airplane tickets to travel to their home countries. Her personal maid, Raymonde, was from France; her butler, Chris, was from England; her chauffeur, Marciano, was from Portugal; one of her maids, Yolanda, was from Italy—and every year, for summer vacation, and occasionally other times, Mrs. Astor would buy them airline tickets so they could fly home. Now, Lourdes was from the Philippines, but she never got a ticket. Lourdes never mentioned it to me but

I wondered, "Why?" I believe it was because she worked in the office with Mr. Marshall and not on a daily basis with Mrs. Astor. I'm sure Mrs. Astor would have been happy to buy her a ticket home at least once every few years had Mr. Marshall said, "Mother, you know Lourdes is from the Philippines; we should give her a ticket too." But he never suggested that, and in all the years I worked at the office, I only recall Lourdes' going home once.

On one of the first days on the job I met Mrs. Astor's then chauffeur, John, who leaned over the seat of the car to shake my hand. "Welcome to the nineteenth century," he said. I wasn't sure quite what he meant, but it foretold a certain way of doing things. Mrs. Astor was from the old school in every way. There was a right way and a wrong way to do things, and the right way had to be *just so*—which usually meant the expensive way.

No one ever saw her leave her apartment without being impeccably dressed, bejeweled, and made up. I once asked her about this, and she told me that everyone she met expected to see "Mrs. Astor," and she couldn't disappoint them. So on most days she wore a suit, her gloves, a beautiful hat, and lovely jewelry—usually a pin, nice earrings, and her three-strand pearls. She always wore her make-up, and I remember that one of the first things she said to me—which she said to just about every new person she met—was, "You know, I've never had a facelift." She always said that. Now, we knew that she had had a little tuck here, maybe a little nip there—but, supposedly, not a full facelift. (The first time I really saw her up close—I had taken something to her office for her to sign—I was looking at her, and thought, "You know, this is really a pretty woman." She was over 90, but she was a pretty woman.) So I asked her, "Without a facelift, what do you do to keep your skin so nice?" And she said, "Well, every night before I go to sleep, when I'm sitting in bed, I push my cheeks up." And she showed me how with the pads of her fingertips she pushed her cheeks up. And I said, "Well, how long do you do that?" And she said, "Until I fall asleep." That made me laugh.

Now to get back to her spending and her clothes, well, they go together. You should note that she went to some event nearly every night (sometimes three in one night!), and she had to be dressed up for those—and during the day she always had a luncheon or a meeting.

Luckily, she loved clothes and she loved to shop. *Loved* to shop. She shopped a lot at Bergdorf Goodman, and she would hit many of the shops up and down Madison Avenue. I know she bought suits at a store called Worldly Things, and she liked Rene Mancini and Helene Arpel for shoes. She'd buy shoes for $400, $500 a pair, and handbags for $1,000, $2,000 each—today they would be three times the price. And she'd buy her books at the Madison Avenue Bookshop. I suspect some of those places went out of business when she stopped shopping!

She would also go to many designer showrooms—Bill Blass, Oscar de la Renta—but she would tell me that when she wanted a really *dressy* dress, she would usually go to Scaasi. Their garments were made of lace and silk, great material, and they were expensive-- $10,000, $12,000, $14,000. It was a joke in the office that we could always tell when Mrs. Astor was having a fitting at Scaasi, because I would immediately get a fax asking me for a 50 percent deposit. We'd laugh. *Whaddaya think, Mrs. Astor is going to abscond and not pay you?* Nobody else ever asked for a deposit, but Scaasi always did. I guess it was the firm's policy.

And then once a year this French designer--I believe it was Balmain--would come to town and usually set up shop at the Plaza Athenee, and she would go and buy a few things. Then the bill would come in, and it was *up* there. I remember Mrs. Astor telling me that Balmain's clothes were beautiful but *"terribly* expensive," so she did understand that they were pricey. But her dear friend Oscar de la Renta had a connection to Balmain, and she wanted to show her support. They'd let her know when they were coming to town, and she'd have some fittings and buy three or four outfits totaling $80,000 or $85,000. I'd have Lourdes pay the bill because she dealt with the foreign money. They wanted to be paid in francs— it wasn't euros yet. Mr. Marshall would definitely grimace when he would see *that* bill!

By the way, Mrs. Astor always wore the Dior perfume Poison, which smelled divine on her. I was reminiscing with Jackie Farrell, the Astor Foundation assistant, about this, and she told me that when Mrs. Astor would come to the office in the winter wearing her fur coat, Jackie would take it to hang up in the closet. Surreptitiously, Jackie would sink her face into the soft mink to get a whiff of the wonderful scent! Even though Jackie is an animal-rights advocate and disapproves of fur coats, she just couldn't help herself.

I thought it was wonderful that this woman, who was well into her nineties, still enjoyed bopping out to the stores and shopping. I know that even at my age I find it tiring to try on clothes, and I get disgusted because things don't fit the way they used to. But Mrs. Astor was always very petite and slim, so clothes looked good on her, and she enjoyed the hunt. Her apartment had the most *beautiful* closets. You'd open one closet and there would be her shoes, just shoes, all lined up and with shoe trees in every one! Each of her outfits was kept in a separate see-through garment bag, and she had a French maid who took care of everything. (Mrs. Astor always said you had to have French maids and English butlers. Old school again.)

Her personal maid, Raymonde Tissot-Bellin, was a young woman in her 30s when Mrs. Astor brought her over from Lyon. She worked for Mrs. Astor for 34 years and took care of every single piece of her clothing. Each morning she would lay out Mrs. Astor's outfit for the day, and she would suggest what jewelry she should wear for which outfit, which hat, which gloves—everything. And when Mrs. Astor traveled, Raymonde would pack her clothes--all these beautiful dresses with matching shoes and bags and hats and gloves--incredible! Raymonde traveled the world with Mrs. Astor, she went everywhere with her, and someone once described them as being like squabbling sisters!

One weekend a funny thing happened. I had been out jogging in Central Park with my sister, Susan, and when we were walking home, crossing Park Avenue, I bumped into Raymonde. She looked stunning. She's an attractive woman to begin with—petite, dark hair, beautiful skin—but every time I had seen her she'd been in the apartment wearing her little French maid's uniform. Today she had on a smashing Yves St. Laurent red suede coat with fur trim. I introduced her to my sister, and then I said, "Raymonde, that's the most stunning coat I've ever seen!" And she said. "You know, I can't wear my clothes in front of Mrs. Astor, so I only wear them on weekends when she is up in the country."

You see, Raymonde lived in the apartment; she had no expenses, so she must have spent her salary on clothes. She had exquisite taste and the most beautiful clothes, many from the French couture houses, but she could wear them only when Mrs. Astor was away. She could not upstage Mrs. Astor. Anyway, seeing her deploy her style sense on her own behalf was an eye-opener. Raymonde retired at the end of 2001 when she turned 70. I think it was a big loss for Mrs. Astor, but the job was just too much for Raymonde then, and she wanted to go home to France.

Sometimes Mrs. Astor would say something nice about my clothes, and I thought it was the greatest compliment, coming from her, a fashion plate. She would look at me and say, "Alice, you look *snappy*! You're a snappy dresser!" I always enjoyed that. Anyway, on one of the days I filled in for her social secretary at the apartment office—I'd been working there for a few years at the time—here came Mrs. Astor down the stairs carrying a suit. Stopping before me she asked, "Alice, would you like this suit? I don't wear it anymore, but it's really very versatile." So I said, "Sure. I'd love it!" And she said, "You know, I think it will fit you." I'm thinking to myself, *This is going to fit me if I have to kill myself. I'll starve myself, but I'll be wearing that suit!* It was a black-and-white, polka-dot suit, silk, Bill Blass, made for her. It was *snug*, but I got into it, and I wore it several times. I still have it, and hope I will fit into it again one of these days! Of course, I sent Mrs. Astor a thank you note and I received a wonderful response back from her, displayed on the next page.

778 Park Avenue

April 17, 1996

Dear, dear Alice

    So many thanks for your very
sweet note. It pleases me very much
indeed that you can wear my dress and
I hope that you have many good times
wearing it.

    I am off, as you know, tomorrow
but will be back, God willing, May first,
so I hope to see you after that.

    With again, so many thanks for
all you do for me.

after
With admiration and affection

Brooke Astor

We were about the same height, same size, but she's very narrow; I think I'm wider in the hip area. Fit often depends on the material and who made the piece—as I found out when I inherited another suit from her by way of Linda Gillies. Mrs. Astor had given a suit to Linda, but it didn't fit her, so Linda called Mrs. Astor and asked whether it would be okay if she passed it on to me. Mrs. Astor said, "Sure." Linda called me about it, and I asked, "Well, what size is it?" And Linda said, "Mrs. Astor's size." You see, many of Mrs. Astor's clothes were handmade for her dimensions. It was a beautiful blue brocade suit made by Oscar de la Renta—magnificent—and it fit me. Another time Mily de Gernier, Mrs. Astor's devoted housekeeper, called me. Mrs. Astor had given her a dressy pants-and-top outfit, but it didn't fit her. Mily had taken it home for her daughter Diane to try on. Didn't fit her either, so Mily said, "Maybe it will fit you." Bingo! So now I have three outfits that were Mrs. Astor's that fit me perfectly. I could fit into all her clothes. Lucky me!

But Mrs. Astor's spending on clothes, on her shopping, on little gifts to the staff and whatnot, seemed to annoy her son no end. Mr. Marshall was always trying to discourage his mother from spending her money. I don't recall the exact figures, but her personal investments at that time totaled at least $60 million, and she lived off the income from the Vincent Astor Trust which was also $60 million. These days, when there are so many billionaires around, that's not an outrageous amount, but it's still a lot of money. Mrs. Astor, however, had no idea whether she was spending a lot or a little.

When I first started working there, one of the first things Mr. Marshall told me was, "Don't ever send my mother anything of a financial nature. She just doesn't understand it." So I didn't. I never showed her any figures. I just assumed that she didn't want to deal with them. She trusted her son; he was taking care of her finances; she didn't need to know. And what I think happened over the years is that she really didn't have any understanding. She didn't know whether $10,000 was a lot of money or a little money. Well, it is all relative, isn't it?

Every now and then she'd call me up, and she would say, "Alice, am I spending too much money? Tony says I'm spending too much money." She'd be agitated, and I'd try to reassure her. "No, Mrs. Astor, you're doing fine. You have lots of money. Mr. Marshall just *worries.*" That's how I covered for him, because I couldn't understand why he said such things. She could live forever and not go through all her money. But this went on from my very arrival there, and it was an uncomfortable situation for me. I was never present when Mr. Marshall told Mrs. Astor that she was spending too much money, but I know it happened all the time. The butler or the chauffeur would call me and say, "Would you please tell Mrs. Astor she has plenty of money, because she's very nervous. Mr. Marshall tells her she's spending too much." He did tell me once that more money was going out than was coming in—but I did not see how that could be. He must have been referring to just the income from the Vincent Astor Trust. So I wound up in the middle of all this—trying to play to the needs of mother *and* son. He would see much of what she spent as wasteful, and she was a woman in her nineties trying to enjoy the last years of her life.

Then one day, this would have been in the late 1990s, Mr. Marshall walked into the office and he said to me flippantly, "Did you tell my mother she wasn't spending *enough* money?"

I said, "What!?"

He said, "My mother said to me that you told her she wasn't spending enough money."

I said, "Oh, Mr. Marshall, I think she must have misinterpreted what I said. Your mother often asks me if she's spending *too much* money, and I always say, 'Of course not. It's your money.' It's not my place to tell Mrs. Astor she's spending too much. I don't know what you want me to say to her." He then just kind of brushed the matter off, as if it were a joke, but I'm thinking, *Why do you do this to your mother? She's old! Why can't she spend her money?* Well, now I suspect I know why. Because he probably believed at that time that soon he would be living off of a trust fund left to him by his mother, so the more money she did not spend, the more money he would inherit. I didn't realize this at that time.

Mrs. Astor would get so rattled about "Tony" telling her she was spending too much money that every now and then she'd sell something. She'd auction off a piece of jewelry or artwork at Christie's because she wanted to go shopping.

Early on I surmised that this mother/son relationship was peculiar. I really needed to know as much as possible about each of them to understand what I was dealing with and how I could best serve them both without upsetting either. I could sense that this was a mother who loved her son, but she did not *like* him. And though I do think Mr. Marshall loved his mother, I sensed he did not like her, either. I had to know their histories—and there was a lot to learn.

—◦◦◦—

CHAPTER THREE

BACKGROUND INFORMATION

———∞∞∞———

I could never have imagined that the sinking of the *Titanic* in 1912 would have such an influence on my life more than 80 years later. But, in fact, if that iceberg had not sunk the *Titanic*, it's very likely that what I am telling you would not have happened, because the Astor fortune surely would have been distributed differently if other children had been born as heirs.

You see, John Jacob Astor IV, who was the great-grandson of the original John Jacob Astor who made the family fortune in fur trading and New York real estate, was traveling back to New York from London with his young second wife, Madeleine Force, on the *Titanic*. She was pregnant, and she survived. He did not. Since her husband did not get back to

New York to change his will, most of his fortune went to his son, Vincent, from his first marriage. He did leave his daughter Alice, also from his first marriage, $5 million, and his will stipulated that $3 million would go to any of his "issue" that survived him other than Vincent and Alice.

When I started my job I knew Mrs. Astor was not an "Astor" by birth, but became one through her third—and final—marriage, to the eccentric and vastly wealthy Vincent Astor. Like most New Yorkers, I was aware of her fame and her charitable work, but I knew little of the woman herself, her character, her family, and her history. So I opened her first autobiography, *Patchwork Child*, the account of her early life that she had signed and given to me at that first Christmas party, and I began to read. Within a few pages, I was enchanted. Brooke Astor was a terrific writer! Under her pen the long-vanished world of her childhood in the early 1900s came vibrantly alive, and the happenings of 90 years ago seemed as exotic and remote as those of the Middle Ages. I would go on to read her second autobiography, *Footprints*, which took me through her marriage to Vincent Astor. Now I had good background information about her life and her relationships.

Few can boast a childhood as varied and interesting as hers. She was born Roberta Brooke Russell on March 30, 1902, in Portsmouth, New Hampshire, the only child of John Henry Russell, an Annapolis graduate, and Mabel Cecile Hornby Howard. She was not from a wealthy background, but she was certainly upper-middle class, and she had a privileged childhood. Her father was a career military officer who became Commandant of the Marine Corps. By her own account, Brooke adored her parents and had a very happy childhood. She loved to read and write and was very curious about everything.

However, it wasn't always an easy existence. Soon after Brooke's birth, her father was posted overseas, and for the next three years she and her mother lived with her Howard grandparents on N Street in Washington, D.C. When her father returned, the family moved to Annapolis where her father would teach at the U. S. Naval Academy. It was the beginning of a peripatetic life common to military families. There would be many other postings—Honolulu, Panama, Newport, Rhode Island—but by far the experience that would do most to shape Brooke Astor's character was her father's assignment as military attache to the American Legation in Peking (now Beijing). The Russells set sail for China in 1910 and stayed there for more than three years, until her father was summoned back to the States. She devotes much of *Patchwork Child* to her years in Peking, where she learned to speak Chinese, traveled to school daily on her small Mongolian horse, and attended childhood parties with the last emperor of China, Pu-Yi.

When the China interlude ended, the family returned to Washington, D.C. where Brooke spent her adolescence attending private school, first Miss Madeira's school and then Holton-Arms.

Because of her love of China, the Astor Foundation, back in the late 1970's, arranged for artisans to come to New York City from China to build the Astor Court at the Metropolitan Museum of Art. It is a replica of a courtyard at the Garden of the Fisherman's Net in Suzhou, a city of such scholars' gardens about an hour's drive from Shanghai. My husband and I traveled to Suzhou in 2000 specifically to see the garden. There I stood with a photograph in my hand of the replica from the Met, and was thrilled to be observing the original. A young Chinese woman walked up to me and, pointing at the photograph, said, "Yes, you are here." She was a guide and was aware of the copy of the garden at the museum.

Joe and Alice Perdue, Suzhou, China

Brooke Russell married for the first time at the very young age of 17, when she was a self –admitted "inexperienced child." The event that led to her betrothal was an invitation to the Commencement Prom at Princeton University. A friend of Brooke's was supposed to go to the dance, accompanying her own brother, but at the last minute came down with the measles. The ill girl's mother implored Brooke's mother to let Brooke fill in. After much debate and then preparation, Brooke was allowed to attend, and that's where she met John Dryden Kuser, of Bernardsville, New Jersey, the son of a very wealthy family with many peculiarities.

They married in April of 1919 at St. John's Episcopal Church in Washington. She was in over her head, and he turned out to be an abusive alcoholic. The marriage, which ended in 1929, was a disaster from the start, but it produced her only son and child, Anthony (Tony) Kuser, born on May 30, 1924. I occasionally heard negative comments from Mrs. Astor about Dryden, and I thought this had to impact to some degree how she looked at her son. Did he remind her of his father? A gesture, a habit? Did Tony think he reminded his mother of a man she disliked? I wondered.

Brooke Russell Kuser next wed Charles Henry (Buddie) Marshall, to whom she stayed married for 20 years--until he died in her arms on Thanksgiving Day 1952, at their country home in Tyringham, Massachusetts.

Buddie was a Wall Street investor who was a senior partner in the firm Butler, Herrick & Marshall. Mrs. Astor often said he was the love of her life. Buddie was more of a father to Tony than his own father, who had had little to do with him. So Tony changed his last name to *Marshall* when he was a teenager. But he was never legally adopted by Buddie, who had two of his own children from his prior marriage.

I got the feeling that Mrs. Astor was not the motherly type. She was more interested in being out and about, participating in the social whirl, than being a hands-on mom. Tony was primarily raised by a nanny and sent off to boarding schools. Mrs. Astor's character of being curious and engaged was not in her son's genetics. Tony dropped out of high school to join the Marines and fought at Iwo Jima in World War II. However, in order to be commissioned as an officer, he needed a high school diploma. His grandfather (Mrs. Astor's father) wrote the headmaster at the Brooks School in Andover, Massachusetts which Tony had attended, and talked him into delivering the necessary paper. The only man I ever heard Mr. Marshall speak lovingly of was his grandfather, whose portrait Tony kept over his desk in the office.

The widow Brooke Marshall then met Vincent Astor. She was invited to a dinner party at which she was seated across from Vincent. Vincent was married at the time to his second wife, Minnie (Cushing), but Minnie wanted a divorce, which Vincent would grant her only if she found him a replacement.

Brooke fit the bill, and she and Vincent Astor married on October 8, 1953 when Mrs. Astor was 51.

The marriage lasted five and a half years, until Vincent, a heavy smoker, died of a heart attack in February 1959 at the age of 67. As a young man of 19, Vincent had had to drop out of Harvard to take over the family business when his father died on the *Titanic*. Vincent had been married twice before his marriage to Brooke but had no children. He had a reputation as a very dour person who did not like socializing, and he and Tony did not get along. They vied for Mrs. Astor's attention, as Brooke found her way into the world of the very, very rich.

The Astor wealth certainly was the largest family fortune ever founded on a rodent. The original John Jacob Astor was born in 1763, the son of a butcher, in Waldorf, Germany. He came to New York after the American Revolution and eventually set up his own fur- trading company. The beaver was the company's primary prey from which John Jacob Astor amassed a small fortune--and turned it into a great fortune. The Astor family crest, a beaver, can still be seen at the Astor Place subway stop in Manhattan. Astor astutely invested his money in New York real estate; when he died in 1848 he owned a great deal of Manhattan, and was said to be the richest man in America.

Later generations of Astors went on to build New York's luxurious mansions and hotels, including the Waldorf-Astoria, which had several incarnations before reaching its present site at 50th Street and Park Avenue. One branch of the family returned to England, where members used their wealth to buy into the English aristocracy. In late nineteenth century Manhattan, Caroline Schermerhorn Astor—*the* Mrs. Astor—ruled society, compiling her list of "the 400"—those people rich and prominent enough to be admitted to her famous ballroom. Caroline's son was John Jacob Astor IV, who married a Philadelphian heiress, Ava Lowle Willing.

Vincent was born to John Jacob and Ava in 1891; his sister, Alice, followed in 1902. But Vincent's parents were unaffectionate and distant, and their marriage ended in divorce, freeing John Jacob to marry the aforementioned much-younger woman, 18-year-old Madelene Force—a short marriage that ended on the *Titanic* after the newlyweds had enjoyed a long honeymoon in Europe. Since Vincent inherited the bulk of the family fortune from his father and had no children, his third wife, Brooke, ultimately ended up with the Astor money.

After Tony left the Marine Corps, Mrs. Astor helped get him into Brown University, from which he graduated. In *Footprints*, Mrs. Astor twice refers to Tony as a "wretched" student. This could not have gone over well with Tony. Can you imagine your mother's telling this to the world? She did not soft-pedal her feelings.

Tony married his first wife, Elizabeth Cryan, while still a student at Brown; they had twin sons, Philip and Alec. The parents divorced when the boys were about seven years old. Tony then married Thelma Hoegnell, known as Tee, and they spent many years overseas, Tony working for the State Department. He was an Ambassador to Kenya, to Trinidad & Tobago, and to the Malagasy Republic. They returned to the US in 1977, and Tony took over running his mother's business office and overseeing her investments in 1979. He divorced Tee after 30 years (no children) to marry his third and present wife, Charlene Gilbert, in 1992. Charlene, who is 21 years younger than Tony, had been the wife of Mrs. Astor's minister in Northeast Harbor, Maine. Mrs. Astor was mortified when Charlene left the minister and their three children to run off with her son. This did not endear Charlene to Mrs. Astor.

So we have three marriages for Brooke, three for Tony, and three for Vincent. It seems that the old expression, "the third one's the charm" holds some weight in this family.

By the time I came on board at the office, Mr. Marshall had been married to Charlene for not quite two years. I slowly learned about their courtship through gossip from other people. The story I was told by Sgt. Carmen Fasciani, a former policeman who functioned as an estate manager and over-saw security at Holly Hill, was that Charlene would parade back and forth in front of Mrs. Astor's house in Northeast Harbor, Maine and obviously had her eye out for Tony. I had sympathy back then for Charlene—she was down-to-earth, friendly, and didn't put on airs—yet!

But I also understood Mrs. Astor's embarrassment and suspicion. What did this much younger woman want with Tony? Mrs. Astor probably saw dollar signs. She often commented to me that Tony was running around too much because he had a younger wife who had never been anywhere or done much. Or she'd tell me that Charlene dressed so "queerly." It was obvious that Mrs. Astor did not like Charlene and vice versa. In fact, Charlene once commented to me that Mrs. Astor never used her name to address her--and Charlene took that as an insult. My guess is that she was right.

Mr. Marshall often showed signs of being perturbed when talking about Mrs. Astor—people were interested in her and asked many questions. Mr. Marshall wanted to talk about himself. He must have fought this focus on his mother for his entire adult life. As soon as people knew he was the son of Brooke Astor, they were curious about *her*, not about him. He wanted to make a name for himself, so he wrote books, and he was on the board of many major New York insti-tutions, thanks to his mother. But none of those activities seemed to distinguish him.

Finally, he was introduced to a legitimate Broadway producer, David Richenthal, and he and Charlene became producers and "Tony" winners. Mr. Marshall had produced a play many years ago but the show, *Alice In Wonderland*, was a flop. This time, he brought money to a terrific cast and an experienced partner, and a hit was born. Their revival of *Long Day's Journey Into Night*, with Vanessa Redgrave and Brian Dennehy, won the Marshalls a Tony Award in 2003. Then they produced their second hit, *I Am My Own Wife*, which won a Tony in 2004. The Marshalls were walking on air, so satisfied with their newfound celebrity. The razzle, dazzle of Broadway seemed to me to change their perception of themselves--Charlene in particular. She was now a Broadway producer, playing with the big boys, thanks again to Mrs. Astor's money.

It is important to understand how, after Vincent died in 1959, his fortune was distributed. About $60 million went to the Vincent Astor Foundation which Mrs. Astor oversaw as president. This money was given away as grants over the next forty years, almost exclusively to New York City institutions. Another $60 million was put into a trust fund, the interest of which Mrs. Astor was to live off of for the rest of her life. When she died, that $60 million would also go to the charities of her choosing. In addition, there was about $2 million in cash that went to Mrs. Astor directly along with most of Vincent's personal property. The cash and personal property are what grew into what was in 2007, at the time of her death, her estate of about $130 million (investments and property). Most of the articles that I have read completely confuse the different entities.

Vincent's half brother, John Jacob Astor VI, who survived the *Titanic* in his mother's womb, sued Mrs. Astor for part of the estate when Vincent died, but he had to settle for a payment of $250,000. It should be noted, however, that John Jacob Astor VI did receive, on his twenty-first birthday, $3 million from the estate of his late father.

The Vincent Astor Foundation was Mrs. Astor's focus from the time of Vincent's death until she closed it to the public at the end of 1997. She had to wrestle with the men who ran the foundation during Vincent's lifetime to gain control, but she won, and went on to become a legend in philanthropic circles. She loved being in a position to make a difference in the lives of New Yorkers. She believed that since the Astor money had been made in New York City, it should be spent in New York City. She also insisted that she actually *see* where the money was to go and how it would be used before a grant was made. So she was known for climbing over all sorts of treacherous construction sites in her beautiful attire and meeting with the responsible parties to which a grant was being made.

After the Vincent Astor Foundation was closed to the public and its office dismantled, Mr. Marshall kept $2 million aside so Mrs. Astor could continue to make small grants as she saw fit. I was selected to oversee the administration of the grants. Before Linda Gillies and her assistant, Jackie Farrell, left in early 1998, they instructed me well on how to proceed when a grant was going to be given. Basically, Mrs. Astor or Mr. Marshall would decide to give a grant to an institution—we no longer would take applications from the public—and I would work with the lawyer, accountant and grantee to follow through the steps required before writing the check. I enjoyed learning something new, and it was satisfying to see a worthy institution get some money. The Vincent Astor Foundation remained open until the end of 2002, when I prepared all the paperwork necessary to close it, sent the documents off to the lawyers and accountants, and wrote the final check, which went to the American Museum of Natural History.

The interesting thing was that the Marshalls benefited from those final grants. Many were given to projects they were interested in and that, therefore, enhanced their social status. I do not bemoan any of the institutions getting grants—they need the money. But later on I will recount Charlene's attitude about the foundation's last years as she herself described them. She spoke during the question-and-answer period after a talk given in December 2007 by Frances Kiernan, Mrs. Astor's biographer, at the Barnes and Noble store across from Lincoln Center. I was in the audience--and how I had to hold my tongue!! I didn't want to put any additional stress on Frances, who had spoken to the crowd while watching Charlene Marshall in the audience furiously scribbling notes.

CHAPTER FOUR

HER LIFESTYLE

—⦇⦈—

When Brooke Marshall married Vincent Astor she suddenly was elevated to the highest rung of New York society. When they first married they lived at the St. Regis Hotel-- which Vincent owned and his father had built in 1904--while their apartment at 120 East End Avenue, at 85th Street, was being renovated. After Vincent died in 1959, Mrs. Astor bought the duplex apartment at 778 Park Avenue, at 73rd Street where she lived for the rest of her life. After her death, her estate sold the apartment in 2011 for a reported $21 million. That's the place I used to visit when I needed her attention for something, or when she wanted me to deal with her jewelry, or to help her if her social secretary was away.

In the late 1990s, we had to replace her entire, antiquated phone system. Her then-secretary, Jolee Hirsch, and I did a thorough evaluation of all the phones in the apartment; many barely worked. Even after the new system was in place, Mrs. Astor kept her old dial princess phone with her private telephone number. She was most comfortable using that one.

The first time I rode up in the elevator to her apartment on the sixteenth floor, I remember thinking that many famous people had been on this elevator and entered her apartment, as I was about to do. I walked into a large reception area and was immediately impressed by the doors leading off to the dining room and living room--black lacquer screens decorated with Chinese figures. The large dining room, only used for entertainment, was to the left; according to Mily, Mrs. Astor's housekeeper, it accommodated either one long table of 22 or three round tables of 8. The walls were covered in large panels of red figures and flowers, reminding me somewhat of the style of the Fragonard room at the Frick Museum.

Opposite the entrance to the apartment was the living room-- quite large, with several seating areas and many paintings, including a few Tiepolos, and the 1878 Lucius Rossi painting of the Astor family. To the right was the gorgeous red-lacquered library, off of which is a terrace facing south and east. Along the south side of the building was "the nook," an area that used to be a stairway down to the fifteenth floor, redone as a small sitting room. That was followed by her den, where she spent most of the time in her last years sitting on the sofa. Down a long hall (off of which was a staircase down to the fifteenth floor), was her large bedroom--in the southwest corner of the building—decorated very femininely in pink. There was a single canopied bed, a fireplace, and a dressing room that led into the bathroom.

The kitchen was large and set up for catering. It led to another work room that led to the formal dining room on one side. On the other side of the kitchen was a small dining room for the staff, and a hallway off of which there were three maid's quarters. Everywhere in the apartment were books, paintings, photographs, figurines, etc.—the collections of her life.

Mrs. Astor divided her time between her three homes—her New York apartment; her 65- acre country estate, Holly Hill, overlooking the Hudson River in Briarcliff Manor, just north of the city; and Cove End, her home in Northeast Harbor, Maine. Each place was wonderful in its own way, but she did much of her entertaining at her apartment in New York. If you had a list of everyone who attended Mrs. Astor's dinners over the years, you would have a list of nearly every notable person who lived, worked in, or visited New York City. Those invitations were coveted. The Kissingers were frequent guests, as were the David Rockefellers; Barbara Walters was a close friend and came often. In earlier years, long before my employment, the Reagans were guests. In later years, Mrs. Astor really liked to have Kofi Annan, the Secretary-General of the United Nations, and his wife as dinner guests. (I was told Harry Belafonte was another favorite—he and Mrs. Astor would sing duets together.)

But these dinners weren't just for fun. When she invited someone to her apartment, there often was a purpose—to raise money for a museum or cause, to introduce people to each other, or to provoke conversation about whatever issue interested her. Who sat next to whom at dinner was very important, and much thought was given to it. (I recall one phone conversation Mr. Marshall was having with Mrs. Astor on the seating topic—it was intense, and amused me!) Mrs. Astor liked to get conversation going, and she was good at it. She would ask provocative questions—or just throw out a topic for everyone to talk about. She liked to hear everyone's opinions about things. An example from my personal experience: I was having lunch with Mrs. Astor at the Knickerbocker Club and she asked my opinion of Mayor Giuliani. I told her I thought he had done a lot of good for the city so I was pleased with him. She agreed that he was a very good mayor, but she said, he needed to improve his manners! It seems she had recently been to a luncheon where the then-mayor sat next to her, and across the table from her sat her dear friend David Rockefeller. At first, the mayor was chatting with Mrs. Astor. But then, he turned his back to her to talk with the person on his other side. This was a no-no. She said she and Mr. Rockefeller exchanged knowing glances! So, Mr. Giuliani, take a tip from Mrs. Astor and polish your manners. Never turn your back on a dinner companion!

According to *The New York Times*, Mrs. Astor's apartment is in one of the most prestigious co-ops in Manhattan. It is one of those old-line, white-gloved-doorman buildings where you need at least $100 million before the board will consider letting you buy an apartment. Mrs. Astor originally had two entire floors—the fifteenth and the sixteenth—but she sold more than half of the fifteenth floor years ago. (You know who bought it? Roone Arledge, the ABC News chairman, and he lived there until he died.) But she did keep a large office on the fifteenth floor, a big room with a fireplace, that was her social secretary's office, and there was also a smaller room as well as a couple of bathrooms and some closets for storage. She originally used the living room on the fifteenth floor for dinner-dances—a sort of ballroom. And when Mrs. Astor's mother was alive, her living quarters were on the fifteenth floor.

Mrs. Astor lived on the sixteenth floor, and her apartment was glorious--nothing splashy, nothing dramatic, but elegant and understated. There were at least a dozen rooms on that floor, including the three maids' rooms, but what I always thought was interesting was that there was no guest bedroom in the entire apartment. Mrs. Astor's bedroom was the only bedroom. There were other rooms that could have been bedrooms. There was one downstairs that Raymonde used for ironing, and it had a bathroom, and that could have been a guest room. Mrs. Astor's social secretary's office was very large with a bathroom off of it, so there was lots of space if she had wanted guest rooms. But I think Mrs. Astor just wanted her privacy. So when she had guests, she put them up elsewhere. They would stay at the Colony Club, the Knickerbocker Club or the Lotos Club.

Most days Mrs. Astor would rise between 9 and 10 a.m. and have her breakfast—she always had a cup of warm water with lemon juice—while Raymonde checked her schedule for the day and laid out her clothes. A few days a week, she had a private yoga lesson at her apartment in the morning.

Once Mrs. Astor was dressed and made up, Marciano, her chauffeur, would pick her up in her Lincoln Town Car and they would begin her rounds. It was always exciting when she'd come to our business office 20 blocks downtown at 54th and Park. In the first few years I was there, she would sometimes bring her dogs, Dolly and Maizie—Dolly was a dachshund and Maizie was a schnauzer—and the whole office seemed to perk up when she was there. Dolly always made her way into my office from the foundation and demanded attention. Maizie was more laid-back and let Dolly take the lead.

Mrs. Astor was just a whirlwind of activity, and she loved to chat. She always found a way to put a smile on your face. A small "for-instance:" In September of 1997, my husband, Joe, and I were planning a vacation to Paris and Provence, and we were going to stay in a small town near Avignon called

Villeneuve-les-Avignon. Mrs. Astor heard about my trip, and it turned out she had once stayed in the same town. So she came into my office with Linda Gillies and they start to sing a little French song about the bridge in Avignon.

> *Sur le pont d'Avignon, l'on y danse, l'on y danse*
> *Sur le pont d'Avignon, l'on y danse, tous en ronde.*
> (translation: On the bridge in Avignon, everyone is dancing in a circle.)

Later, I left her and Linda at the elevator, and when I got back, there was a Post-It note on my seat saying, "Have a great trip!" It was just so funny and sweet of her. I'll never forget 95-year-old Mrs. Astor singing to me about the bridge in Avignon.

If she had her dogs with her, Marciano would take her to Rockefeller University, Carl Schurz Park, or Central Park so she could walk Dolly and Maizie,--or, years later, Boysie and Girlsie. Marciano always looked out for her. He was devoted to her, and extremely protective. But she had a habit of taking off and walking by herself. Sometimes, if the car was stuck in traffic, she'd get impatient and say, "I'm going to get out and walk." Her prior chauffeur, John Meany, once called me, and he was frantic. "Have you heard from Mrs. Astor?" he yelled. "I've lost her! She's somewhere in the park, and I can't find her! She went into the park with the dogs, and I don't know where she'll come out!"

It always turned out okay, but all the warnings about the dangers of wandering off alone had absolutely no effect whatsoever. She had no fear. She talked to everyone equally—prince or pauper, friend or stranger. People would know she was "someone," but they mostly did not know who she was. I remember one frigid December day when she had gone to have her hair done at Kenneth's in the Waldorf-Astoria and she was supposed to come up to the office later in the day. I was worried about her walking up Park Avenue after her appointment. It was snowy, the sidewalks were treacherous--sheets of ice--and Marciano wasn't scheduled to pick her up that day. I had scary visions of her taking a bone-breaking fall. I was getting more nervous by the minute when suddenly the door opened, and she walked in. I said, "Mrs. Astor! I've been so worried! How did you get here? It's four blocks from the hotel!" And she said, "Oh, I just walked out of the Waldorf and I saw a nice young man walking by, and I just said, 'Do you mind if I hold onto you?' and he walked me here." That's just how she was. She'd talk to anybody. And she had great rapport with everyone.

When you look back, you realize that we really had no security in those pre-9/11 days. Now you've got to practically show the results of a blood test to get into any large building in New York, but back in the '90s there were just the receptionists at the desk downstairs, and that was it. No real security. So occasionally total strangers would tell the desk they had an appointment with Mrs. Astor and just wander up to the office and ring the bell.

We would never let in anyone we didn't know, so they'd leave and that was that. But Mrs. Astor often had meetings with important people at her office, and that was fun for us. One day Charlie Rose, the TV interviewer, came up. She just loved Charlie Rose. She gave money to Channel 13 for his show. And we were all peeking around corners, trying to see Charlie Rose.

I kept files on the nuisance cases—characters who showed up regularly wanting to see Mrs. Astor. There was one person from the South who used to go around telling people he was in business with Mrs. Astor—he used her name in his scams. I had a huge file on him. One day Mr. Marshall got a call from a sheriff in South Carolina who said, "I've got a man sitting across the desk from me, and he claims Mrs. Astor has invested a lot of money in his business. Do you know this man?" That was one of our long-term problems— he kept popping up for years.

There was another person, an artist, who used to send packages of his "artwork" to the office, and I would open it up, and at first I just thought, *This is really strange.* It was just crazy artwork, but each package he sent would get more and more erotic. I made sure Mrs. Astor never saw any of it, but we had to keep a file on him--so his work is probably still preserved in storage somewhere!

One time a man rang the bell and presented me with a postage stamp from Micronesia with Mrs. Astor's image on it. He was a stamp collector and wanted to get an autograph. I sent the stamp to Mrs. Astor and she kindly accommodated his request.

So you had to be really wary about people who would call, but at the same time you never knew when something strange might be legitimate. One day in August 1999, I was sitting at my desk, and I got a call from London. A man's voice said, "Hello, I'm the social secretary for Prince Charles." And I was about to say, "And I'm Queen Elizabeth," but luckily I didn't. He went on to say that on her last visit to London Mrs. Astor had told Prince Charles—they were great friends—that she would like to give a luncheon for Camilla Parker Bowles whenever she came to New York, and Camilla was coming in September.

At the time Mrs. Astor was at her Maine estate for the summer, her social secretary was on vacation--everybody was away, which is why the call came to me at the business office-- and so I just said, "Let me take down the information, and I'll get back to you." Because Mrs. Astor was off in Maine, she asked her friend Barbara Walters to handle the guest list for the luncheon, which was to be held in Mrs. Astor's Park Avenue apartment.

Then came the deluge. Even though our office telephone number was unlisted, somehow the British press got the number, and I was just *flooded* with calls. You know how aggressive those British tabloids are, and I would get a barrage of questions. "Who's going to be invited? What are they going to wear? Who will sit next to Camilla? Who's catering the luncheon?" And on and on and on. And I would just say, "This is Mrs. Astor's business office. I really have no knowledge of the luncheon." I was at my wit's end when yet another British journalist called. "Oh, you must be getting calls from everybody," he said. And I said, "I am, and I really have nothing to tell any of you because I don't work in the apartment. I work in the business office, and I have nothing to do with the luncheon." But he was very nice, and we chatted. Then we chatted some more. And some more. And then I said, "I'm very sorry I can't help you." And at the end he said, "Wait! Wait! So you really have no idea what kind of canapés they're serving?" It was his last attempt—anything! Get me a little something! It was very funny and pathetic.

The luncheon made a splash even in the New York papers, but I think Mrs. Astor was a little flummoxed by it. As I said, Barbara Walters was in charge of the guest list, and so it included a lot of showbiz people. One couple I remember was the actor Michael Douglas and his wife, the actress Catherine Zeta-Jones. Maybe they were included because Catherine Zeta-Jones is a British subject, and Barbara Walters might have thought that made for something in common with Camilla. Anyway, Mrs. Astor's secretary, Jolee, later told me Mrs. Astor looked around the room and said, "Who *are* these people?" They just weren't from her circle.

Her friendship with Prince Charles was deep and long-standing--a very close relationship. She used to go to London twice a year or so, and she'd often see the prince. I recall one time he wanted her to see his gardens, so he picked her up in London in his helicopter and flew her to his palace at Highgrove. They both were tremendously interested in gardens, and that was one bonding of their common interests. So they had lunch, then a garden tour, and then he helicoptered her back to London. All in one day.

Mrs. Astor always loved flowers, *loved* flowers. Her apartment had fresh flowers in every room all the time (we spent about $4000 to $6000 on flowers each month in the city), and at her Holly Hill estate in Westchester and at Cove End in Maine she had acres of gardens, greenhouses, and cutting beds. I'll get to that soon, but let me tell a little more about Prince Charles and the royal family.

This tale had been told to me by one of her dear friends. Years ago, at an evening benefit at Lincoln Center, Mrs. Astor was sitting next to Prince Charles at dinner when he had just become engaged to Lady Diana Spencer. At an earlier meeting with the prince that same day, Mrs. Astor happened to be wearing a beautiful pin of precious stones in the shape of a bird. "Oh, what a lovely pin," Prince Charles said to her. That night, Mrs. Astor handed a beautifully wrapped box to Prince Charles, and said, "Why don't you give this to your

Princess?" I can absolutely see Mrs. Astor doing that, and I'm sure it endeared her to him. In the box was the pin.

I never heard Mrs. Astor talk about Diana, even though I'm sure she knew her. She never mentioned Camilla either, for that matter. But she definitely felt close to Prince Charles, and I know why--because Mrs. Astor was interested in *men*. She didn't like it when she would hear people talking about this, but Mrs. Astor was known as a flirt. A *big* flirt. And she *loved* to have men around.

She told me a story once, when we were having lunch at the Knickerbocker Club. She was attending a very posh event in England, and one of the guests was the Queen Mum—Queen Elizabeth's mother—and the proceedings just dragged on and on. The Queen Mum was getting bored and seemed so restless she might get up and leave. Of course, that would have been a social disaster, and the head of the event didn't know what to do. So Mrs. Astor leaned over and made a suggestion. "Have a few of the men take the Queen Mum for a stroll around the grounds," she said. Well, they did that, and the Queen Mum *loved* it and stayed the whole time. She wanted *attention*. And the attention of *men*. Now, the Queen Mum was quite elderly at the time, but that didn't matter. And Mrs. Astor was the same way—so she *knew*. As soon as those men talked to her, took her for a walk, paid attention, the Queen Mum was interested and hung around-- and Mrs. Astor saved the day.

A branch of the Astor family had returned to England years before, and many Astors still live there, so Mrs. Astor always had a full social calendar during her visits to England. Even into her late nineties, every day was packed—luncheons, dinners, parties, country weekends...you name it. When she went to England she'd stay a week or 10 days, and she always took a suite at the Connaught in Mayfair. She flew on the Concorde or first-class on British Airways, always accompanied by Raymonde. (Almost every time, though, she'd forget something—a favorite nightgown or whatever—and we'd have to FedEx it over.) She would often visit with the Marquess and Marchioness of Salisbury at their home, Hatfield House. And, although the story has been told by many, you may not have heard it. Mrs. Astor was staying at Hatfield House, one of the grandest houses in Hertfordshire, and was reading in bed at night when she heard the dogs barking. She thought her hosts had forgotten to let them in, so she got up and was making her way to the outside door when all the lights in the house went out and it was pitch-black. She had to crawl on the floor until she found a doorknob, let herself into a room, and found a bed to sleep in for the rest of the night. Mrs. Astor told me this story while I was lunching with her at her apartment. A day later the tale was in the newspaper (she must have shared it with several other people besides me). It seems all the lights go out automatically at 10:00 p.m. at Hatfield House!

As I have mentioned, she always maintained that it was best to have French maids and English butlers, and her butler at Holly Hill was Christopher Ely, an Englishman. Chris, a no-nonsense man, was totally devoted to her. He was very protective and always tried to please her. On her weekends up there he would drive her around to any place she wanted to go—and he always made sure everything was just so.

During Mrs. Astor's tenure, Holly Hill, a stately old stone house overlooking the Hudson River, was beautiful beyond beautiful. The house, which wasn't huge, was set behind walls; you approached the property through a gate, and there was a long drive to the entrance. There was a guesthouse, a greenhouse and several other buildings on the 65-acre property, which was completely private. From April to autumn, something was blooming and flowering everywhere. Mrs. Astor particularly liked her 40,000 daffodil bulbs. There was both an indoor lap pool and outdoor pool with a pool house. Inside, though it was like a museum given all the photographs of famous people and paintings on the walls, it was a warm and welcoming home. Outside, the grounds were tended by three full-time gardeners and a host of nursery, lawn and tree companies.

I went to Holly Hill only once during the years I was employed in the Astor office. My visit was in the summer of 1996, when the Marshalls were living in the guest house while their apartment was being renovated. My husband and I drove up to deliver some documents and have lunch with the Marshalls at the pool house. We got a tour of the grounds and the guest house, but the main house was closed for the summer.

Left to right: Alice Perdue, Anthony Marshall, Charlene Marshall

In a way, I came to see Holly Hill as Mrs. Astor's refuge. She retreated to this estate when she broke her hip the first time. It happened in 1998, at a fundraising dinner at the American Museum of Natural History on the West Side of Manhattan. She was wearing fairly high heels, and she fell. Well, *panic*. There were lots of doctors there, and they rushed her to New York Hospital. As soon as I heard, I thought, *Oh, my goodness*, because when an older person breaks a hip, that's often the end—and Mrs. Astor was 96! As soon as she could, she got herself to Holly Hill to recuperate.

Now, Mrs. Astor loved to swim, and, as I said, Holly Hill has two pools. About two weeks after she broke her hip, I got a phone call. It was her nurse, Minnette Christie. I had never spoken to her, and yet Minnette called me at the office and said, "You know, I've just got to tell someone about this. Mrs. Astor is such an inspiration to me." And I said, "What do you mean?" And she said, "It's only been two weeks since she broke her hip, and today she said she wanted to go swimming! So I took her to the pool, she got in the water, and started swimming. Now I'm thinking to myself, 'I'm standing here in my nurse's uniform. If anything happens, I'm going to have to jump in and retrieve her!' Well, forget it. The woman is a fish! She just swam back and forth, back and forth. I never had to go in and get her. I can't get over it."

A few days later Mrs. Astor told Minnette she wanted to take a walk around the grounds of Holly Hill, which she had always loved to do. So Minnette got her ready and figured they'd take a little stroll. Well, they headed out, and Mrs. Astor set off across the grounds. They walked and walked, and Minnette told me she started thinking, "What happens if she gets tired? What happens if she can't walk anymore? I'm going to have to *carry* her!" Minnette didn't need to worry. "No problem," she told me over the phone. "We walked for quite a while and I didn't have to help her at all. She walked out, then came all the way back. Fine. I'm just amazed. I'm so amazed at this woman."

By the way, I had sent Mrs. Astor a Beanie Baby dog just to cheer her after her fall—what do you get Mrs. Astor?— and I got the loveliest note back from her, shown on the next page.

I worried about her even years after she had broken her hip. Around Christmastime of 2001, for instance, Mrs. Astor invited Lourdes and me to lunch at the power-broker restaurant the Four Seasons. We arrived first and were shown to our table. (It was actually the architect Philip Johnson's table, but he wasn't dining there that day so we got it!) At the Four Seasons you have to walk up a short flight of stairs, so I'm looking out for her, and, sure enough, here comes Mrs. Astor walking up the stairs with no help, (though her secretary, Birgit, was with her) and coming to our table. She was almost 100 at the time! (I recall she ordered the crab cakes so I did too. Yummy!)

778 Park Avenue

June 30, 1998

Darling Alice,

The little dog came in barking yesterday, so I took him in my hand and he resisted a bit, wanting to sit straight up. I find him a delightful companion, especially since I am without my own dogs, Boysie and Girlsie. A thousand thanks for thinking of me in such a wonderful way.

Gratefully and
with affection

Brooke Astor

It was sheer will, I think. So much that she did was just pure will. She always moved forward. She did not look back. I once read that there's one common thread in the lives of people who live to be very old—they do not wallow in misery or constantly think about their past. They look forward. And that was Mrs. Astor all the time. It was always "What's next on my calendar?" And her calendar had such exciting people and events on it, how could she possibly not go?

We were very worried—particularly Linda Gillies—about what would happen to Mrs. Astor after she closed down the Astor Foundation to the public at the end of 1997. She was always deeply involved in whatever the foundation was sponsoring—visiting projects, talking to people. It was her life. How would she carry on when that was no longer there? Well, it was amazing. She just kept going, going forward. She still had her social life—luncheons, dinners, people coming over for tea. She was still on the boards of museums and whatever, so there were always events.

It got to be kind of a joke around the office—Mrs. Astor's endurance. When I started working there she already was 91, and I remember thinking, *Well, this isn't going to be a long-term job*. Lourdes thought the same thing when she started—Mrs. Astor was 83 then—and Lourdes worked there for almost 22 years! After a while you realized that Mrs. Astor was like the Energizer Bunny—she was just never going to stop! We thought she must have had a magic potion, but all we could come up with was that she took B-12 shots.

Her one weakness was bronchial. She got bronchial infections. Shortly after I started working in her office she made an overnight trip to London. She flew over, went to a party that night, and flew back the next day. How many people in their nineties could do that? Well, she came down with bronchitis, and she was very ill. I thought, *Oh, my God, I just started here, and Mrs. Astor is going to pass away!* She was sick for quite awhile, but she recovered, thank goodness; she was just tough as nails.

But she did slow down a bit as the years went by, and at one point she started to go down to Florida. She would rent a private house and go to Palm Beach. At first in April, which I thought was strange, because it was after the season, and in subsequent years she visited in February. When she flew domestically, she would charter a jet from Wayfarer Ketch, a company owned by the Rockefellers and based at Westchester Airport. She would take Raymonde, her personal maid; Chris Ely, her butler from Holly Hill; another maid; and a cook. Then down in Florida she'd hire whatever additional help she needed, like a laundress. But since she was going for a month or six weeks, she also needed to take a lot of her stuff—her wardrobe, her jewelry, her hats—she even took her own china.

It was quite a sight to see, I was told, when Mrs. Astor arrived at Westchester Airport for her flight. Marciano would drive her and her dogs in one car and she'd rent several other limousines to carry her help and her baggage. All these cars from the city and from Holly Hill would converge at her jet. Mrs. Astor and her dogs would get on the plane and settle in, and then the others would just be *pouring* stuff onto the jet—luggage and bags and boxes and crates and whatever. Then they would all fly down to Palm Beach. But I don't think Mrs. Astor really liked it down there. She usually came back early. After a few weeks of shopping on Worth Avenue, attending a few events, and seeing old friends for lunch and dinner, she would get bored and long for the comforts of her own homes.

Then she would spend her summers in Maine at Cove End. Besides the main house, there was a guest house, a couple of small cottages, a greenhouse and a cutting garden. The property overlooks the cove in Northeast Harbor. Mrs. Astor had five full-time gardeners on her staff there, as well as a year-round housekeeper. In addition, in summer, staffers from the apartment and Holly Hill would alternate at Cove End for the month of July or August, and several temporary people would be hired to help with all the visitors and entertaining.

Mrs. Astor had owned another nearby property in Maine called August Moon, which had a teahouse and a pool where she went to swim. But she sold it in the mid-1990s for not very much money--a million or so--and then she built a pool at Cove End. She loved her summers in Maine, and it's ironic that Cove End then featured so prominently in the problems of her old age.

The first problem was the scandal that rocked Northeast Harbor in 1989 when Mr. Marshall began an affair with Charlene Gilbert. It wasn't only that he was then still married to his second wife, Thelma ("Tee"), but that Charlene was married to Paul Gilbert, the rector of the Episcopal church where Mrs. Astor worshipped every Sunday—St. Mary's-by-the-Sea—and she was the mother of three children! (This was before my employment, but, as I mentioned, I was told by several former employees that Charlene would parade back and forth in front of Mrs. Astor's property hoping to bump into Mr. Marshall.)

Mrs. Astor felt dreadfully embarrassed. Everyone in Northeast Harbor knew about the affair, and Mrs. Astor told friends that she felt she couldn't go to church anymore, she was so embarrassed. Well, of course, she nonetheless still did go to church and kept a stiff upper lip. Later that year Charlene left her husband and her two younger children and moved to New York to be close to Mr. Marshall. Mrs. Astor was horrified.

In May 1992, Mr. Marshall and Charlene got married—I heard that his divorce from Tee came through in the morning, and he and Charlene were married in the afternoon. They moved into a very nice apartment at 79th Street and Lexington Avenue that Mrs. Astor bought for them, and a whole new life began for Charlene.

Now, Mrs. Astor was polite to Charlene, but there was always a coolness in their relationship. For one thing, Charlene was some 21 years younger than Mr. Marshall, and I would guess that Mrs. Astor felt—at least to some degree—that she was marrying him for the money. On many occasions when I was with her, Mrs. Astor would tell me, "You know, Tony married this much younger woman, so now he's running around because she's never done anything before! She was a minister's wife. She'd never traveled, so now they're running around all the time having fun, and he's tiring himself out."

But I've got to say that Charlene was very nice to me, at least in the early days. From the beginning, I was pleasantly surprised that she was so down-to-earth, working full-time then as the executive director of the Garden Club of America, which wasn't far from our office. I thought that was kind of neat—she was just another working woman.
She'd always chitchat with me when she called the office. She was full of life, you know--very talkative and pleasant. When she'd come up to the office with Mr. Marshall or meet him there, we'd fall into conversation--long talks that I don't think Mr. Marshall liked. He'd cut us short, and at that time I felt, *He's the one in charge.* She would talk about her children—she had two girls and a boy—she'd talk about

money—the cost of college loans, other problems, because at that time she probably still didn't feel comfortable that "his money was her money."

I recall being taken out to dinner twice by the Marshalls. Once, Joe and I were invited to their apartment for drinks and then we walked around the corner to a local restaurant for dinner. The second time, we discovered we were both going to the same theatre to see *Smoky Joe's Café*. Joe and I were going for our anniversary, and the Marshalls were going because Mr. Marshall was a Tony voter. So we met for dinner before the show. On both occasions we had a lovely time. Charlene was especially fun and we had lively conversation. But my husband commented to me that Mr. Marshall never asked either of us a personal question. It wasn't a give and take conversation. He talked mostly about himself and his thoughts.

———

Once Mrs. Astor's health began to decline and Charlene began to feel more comfortable in her new world, her demeanor changed. One of the big changes involved Charlene's use of Mrs. Astor's prized jewels-- I'll tell you all about that later. One of the first changes involved Cove End. Charlene and Mr. Marshall would continue to go up to Maine in the summers while Mrs. Astor was there; they stayed in the guesthouse for several weeks, but not the entire summer. Mrs.

Astor would have other guests coming and want the guest-house for them. So the Marshalls had to leave.

I know that Mrs. Astor had at one time intended to leave the guest cottage to Philip, her grandson, who had spent so many vacations there. Marciano had told me that, while Mrs. Astor and Philip were in the back seat of her car, he had overheard her tell Philip that she wanted to leave him the guest cottage in her will. Philip replied that he was very grateful, but he asked that she not do it. He said he'd prefer not to get into a big argument with his father about it.

So it became clear to me that Mr. Marshall coveted Cove End in its entirety. In early 2003 when Mrs. Astor's health was declining, he persuaded her to sign over the Cove End property to him. I don't know how he managed this. He may have told her that for tax reasons this made more sense—if she gave him the property before her death, the amount of the tax would be less than if she left it to him in her will. But several months later, several other employees and I were shocked to learn Mr. Marshall had transferred ownership of the property to Charlene!

Did this raise a few eyebrows? You can imagine. Now the humble minister's wife who for years had lived in the Episcopal minister's parish house had come to own the Astor estate in Northeast Harbor. Cove End would now eventually go to *her* children—and not to the grandchildren of Mrs. Astor herself.

One other note about taxes: I recall Mr. Marshall asking that a check from Mrs. Astor be made out to Charlene in early 2004 as a gift for $11,000; he explained that since Charlene would have to pay the real estate taxes on Cove End, the money would help. Then he asked that a check for $40,000 later that year--around June--be made out to him, again saying they would have to pay the taxes for Cove End that year. I wondered why Mrs. Astor should be responsible for the real estate taxes after the property was transferred to the Marshalls. Besides, the taxes on Cove End at that time were under $30,000, so why did they need a total of $51,000 to pay those taxes? Hmmmm...

CHAPTER FIVE

BAUBLES, BANGLES
AND BULGARI

Charlene's borrowing of Mrs. Astor's best jewels caused a lot of gossip, and I want to set down what I recall about it. Mrs. Astor had beautiful jewelry—and a lot of it— but her two best pieces were (1) her emerald necklace, and (2) a diamond necklace known as the "Snowflake." I think Mrs. Astor was particularly fond of her emeralds because her late husband Vincent Astor had commissioned them from Bulgari shortly before his death. (In fact, I once came across a letter in the files from Bulgari to Mrs. Astor saying, "I'm sure your husband would still want you to have these"—they apparently weren't fully paid for when he died.)

Anyway, everyone knew Mrs. Astor's emeralds. I don't recall exactly what they originally cost but it was over $100,000 in 1959, and they were on Mrs. Astor's insurance policy for over $400,000. She wore them for her formal portraits, and often when she attended a grand event. They're enormous emeralds separated by large diamonds and with a matching pair of earrings that she bought from Verdura. She also had a huge emerald ring—her engagement ring from Vincent—and a large diamond pin with a big emerald in its center. She loved emeralds. All the pieces are absolutely gorgeous!

Bulgari emerald necklace

So it caused quite a stir in social circles when Charlene turned up wearing the emerald necklace at the Tony Awards in 2004.

She and Mr. Marshall won a Tony that year for producing *I Am My Own Wife*, but all anyone could talk about were Mrs. Astor's emeralds around Charlene's neck. No one--but no one-- had ever worn Mrs. Astor's emeralds before. It's a real no- no. Yet when a writer for *Vanity Fair* magazine interviewed Charlene for the December 2006 issue, Charlene claimed that she had gone to Mrs. Astor before the Tony ceremony and asked if she could borrow a piece of jewelry, and Mrs. Astor had said, "Why don't you wear the emeralds?"

My reaction was *BALONEY!* What really happened is that Mr. Marshall went up to his mother's apartment before the Tony Awards in June 2004 and asked to see all her necklaces. He took the emeralds for Charlene to wear. I know this is true because I got a phone call from Mily, Mrs. Astor's housekeep- er, immediately after Mr. Marshall left the apartment with the emeralds. "I'm so upset!" Mily said. "Mr. Marshall just took the emeralds for Mrs. Marshall to wear!" He should not have taken the emeralds—there were plenty of other necklaces he could have chosen. Mily said that Mr. Marshall said to her, "I will feel as though my mother is in attendance at the Tonys if Charlene wears her emeralds!" I gagged.

The prior year it had been almost the same thing. That time the borrowed jewelry had been the "Snowflake" necklace. It's a beautiful diamond necklace that Mrs. Astor bought at Van Cleef and Arpels for $270,000. (Actually, she traded in a piece of jewelry to Van Cleef and Arpels for $250,000 and got the

"Snowflake" in exchange-- and I wrote a check to the jewelry store for the extra $20,000.) Anyway, this was the last big piece of jewelry that Mrs. Astor bought, and I was aware that Mr. Marshall had asked his mother to leave the "Snowflake" to Charlene in her will. He wanted it. He was so possessive of it. One time in early 2003—before she broke her hip for the second time—when Mrs. Astor was going out, she asked to see all her necklaces, most of which were kept in the safe in the office at that time. So I was going to send them up to Mily in the apartment, and I told Mr. Marshall that Mrs. Astor wanted to see her necklaces. And he said to me, "Okay, but do me a favor—don't send up the 'Snowflake.'" And I thought, *Why not? She still owns it.* But I didn't send it.

Van Cleef & Arpels diamond snowflake necklace

So when the Marshalls were nominated for a Tony in 2003 for Best Revival for their production of *Long Day's Journey Into Night*, Charlene turned up at the Tony Awards wearing the "Snowflake." In that same *Vanity Fair* article I mentioned, Charlene said she had gone to Mrs. Astor to borrow a piece of jewelry, and Mrs. Astor had said, "Why don't you wear the 'Snowflake?'" Charlene added that when she brought it back the next day, Mrs. Astor said to her, "You know, I don't wear it anymore. Why don't you keep it?"

Which is again...*BALONEY*! The Tonys take place in June. Charlene did not keep the "Snowflake" right after the Tonys. The "Snowflake" necklace was returned to the office safe. When Mr. Marshall finally took possession of the "Snowflake," he took it from the safe in the office in December of 2003. One day that month, Mr. Marshall asked to see the jewelry that was in the safe, and he took the "Snowflake" and a matching pair of diamond earrings. He told me he was putting them in a safety deposit box in his name, and I could cancel the insurance on the necklace because the "Snowflake" wouldn't be worn. And if it was worn occasionally, he said he could call the insurance company and say, "Insure it for this night." That's what he told me, and I took it off the insurance. That was when he got the necklace, not when Mrs. Marshall returned it to Mrs. Astor after the Tony Awards.

Another piece of jewelry Charlene got from Mrs. Astor was her double-diamond ring. Now this piece is fabulous—and enormous. Each diamond is five carats—so this is a 10-carat double diamond ring. Mrs. Astor gave the ring to Charlene one day when she and Mr. Marshall were visiting her at Holly Hill. I remember because Chris Ely, the butler at Holly Hill, called me and said, "Mrs. Marshall just went *skipping* out of here wearing Mrs. Astor's double-diamond ring!" So she must have given it to her. But then I heard from Chris a few weeks later that Mrs. Astor was saying to herself, "Why did I give that ring away?" She either didn't mean to give it away or couldn't remember. So, who knows? I wasn't there. But what I heard from the staff was that often, when Mrs. Astor had an argument with Tony, she would make up by giving him something. So he would be pleased if Mrs. Astor gave something or showed some kindness to Charlene—but that's quite a ring.

Mr. Marshall never told me to take that ring off of Mrs. Astor's insurance. I don't know why. Maybe they never took it off the insurance because they didn't want to report it as a gift—it had to be worth several hundred thousand dollars—and pay a gift tax. Anyway, the irony was that, at least until Mrs. Astor's estate was settled, the court had made Charlene return all the jewelry that she got from Mrs. Astor as part of the settlement of the guardianship petition filed by Philip in 2006. It was being kept in a safe at JPMorgan Chase. But I had to laugh to myself when, in August 2006, I was called into the Astor office for a few days by Mary Anne Berkery and Louise Mulligan from JPMorgan Chase to help them out. JPMorgan Chase sealed the office, by court order after Philip's petition, and had called in Sotheby's to itemize the jewelry in the office safe and transfer the pieces to a JPMorgan safe downtown.

There were two women there from Sotheby's, people from JPMorgan, and a guard with a gun. There were about 12 pieces, including the emerald necklace, the emerald ring, and a pearl-and-diamond necklace. All this security! This was so funny to me because Mily and I used to carry the jewels in a little sack or a tote bag whenever Mrs. Astor wanted them. If Mrs. Astor wanted a piece from the office safe, I'd put it in a little sack, grab a cab, and take it up to her apartment. Sometimes I would be carrying millions of dollars in jewelry in my little tote bag. I never thought anyone could imagine what I had in my tote, so I always felt safe and didn't think anything about it. Now they had a guy with a gun!

Mily and I were always taking jewelry back and forth from the apartment to the office and vice versa because Mrs. Astor didn't like to travel with her best stuff. When she went to Maine in the summer or to Florida in the winter, she'd send Mily over with the best pieces to be kept in the office safe. She also had a safe in her apartment, and only her two long-time employees—Mily and Raymonde—had access to it. A lot of other pieces were just kept in a dressing-table drawer, and when Mrs. Astor went to Holly Hill on weekends the pieces she wanted to take were packed off with her.

I'll never forget the day I had to take her emerald necklace back to Bulgari. A couple of the stones were missing, and the necklace needed repair. So I put the emeralds in my tote, the chauffeur picked me up, and off we went to Bulgari on Fifth Avenue and 57th Street. When I walked in they were polite but—not overly friendly. You know how those places are— very low-key. But when I whipped out the emeralds from my tote—well—I was suddenly deserving of more attention!! I explained that they were Mrs. Astor's emeralds and they needed some work done on them, and they gave me a receipt stating that the necklace was a very *important* piece. Ahem.

Once a year, in early December, the insurance agent Joe Augello, a tall, nice-looking gentleman, would come to the office to go over the many policy renewals--for homes, furnishings, automobiles, liability, etc.--with Mr. Marshall. The policy for jewelry and fine art was the most interesting, and I enjoyed reviewing it, since each piece was described and valued. I was particularly interested in a painting Mrs. Astor owned by Maurice Prendergast, an artist I love. It hung in the living room at Holly Hill, and I always wanted to see it. Prendergast had painted many beach scenes, including a scene of Nantasket, Massachusetts, where my family had a summer home when I was a child. I finally got to view Mrs.

Astor's Prendergast when I visited her near the end of her life. The painting wasn't of Nantasket though it was called *Low Tide*. I recall it was insured for $200,000.

I got to know Mrs. Astor's jewels very well because of my job handling the insurance, which required that I catalog the pieces. When I first started working in Mrs. Astor's office, there really wasn't any definitive list of what she owned. I had a list of pieces that were insured; two old books of photographs of some pieces; and the jewelry itself, and the three didn't always match. Some pieces had been photographed but weren't insured; others were insured but hadn't been photographed; and then there were others I'd never heard of. So I started going up to Mrs. Astor's apartment to make a complete record.

Now this was *fun*. I'd have Mily or Raymonde get handfuls of Mrs. Astor's jewels and lay them out on her bed, and I'd photograph them. We'd chat and I'd learn the background of some of the pieces, and then I'd take pictures of all this jewelry—and there were some *magnificent* pieces. Then I would go back to the office and try to match things to the insurance list and to the old pictures. So it was quite a job, but it was fun, and eventually I got it pretty much organized. I had a nice folder accounting for all her jewelry.

Anyway, one day in 2002 I was either picking up or delivering a piece of jewelry to her apartment—I forget which—and when I walked in, Mrs. Astor was there. When people were around, Mrs. Astor liked to chat. So we were talking, and Mily was helping me— all kinds of stuff was going on—and Mrs. Astor was sitting at her dressing table getting ready to go to lunch. At one point Mrs. Astor opened a drawer that was full of jewelry, pulled out a strand of pearls, and she said to me, "Would you like these?" Now Mrs. Astor loved to give things away, but this was too much. I thought, *Oh, my God*! What I said was, "Oh, Mrs. Astor those are beautiful!" They were big, baroque pearls (I had even taken a picture of them for the insurance) and I said, "Mrs. Astor, they are really lovely, but why don't you wear them? You should keep them." And she said, "No, no. I have another strand just like it." And she pulled another strand of pearls out of the drawer— she had two of the same. They just had different clasps. I never would have taken them if Mily hadn't been there, because I felt funny about it. You know, someone could accuse me of just taking them. So I said, "Mily, I don't know what to do. Mrs. Astor wants to give me these pearls..." And Mily said, "Well, take them."

So there we were in Mrs. Astor's bedroom, and five minutes later, Mr. Marshall walked in. I immediately said to him— because I still felt funny about it—"Mr. Marshall, your mother just gave me this gorgeous strand of pearls." I could just tell that he wasn't pleased. And then as I was leaving Mrs. Astor grabbed something else from the drawer—it was a pin—and she said, "Why don't you give this to Lourdes?"

Well, Mr. Marshall looked at it, and it was a pin of some kind that the Marine Corps had given her. Mrs. Astor didn't realize it, but it wouldn't have been appropriate to give that to Lourdes, so Mr. Marshall said, "Oh, no, you can't give her that," and he put it back. I thought he was going to suggest that Mrs. Astor give Lourdes something else, but he didn't. Of course, I now felt guilty because I didn't want to go back to the office and tell Lourdes that Mrs. Astor had given me these beautiful pearls but there was nothing for her.

Anyway I did go back to the office, and Mr. Marshall came in a little later. "Oh, Mr. Marshall, I was just so surprised that Mrs. Astor gave me those pearls," I said to him. "I was kind of shocked!" So he said to me, "Why don't you get them appraised?" I said, "Okay," but I was thinking, *What does that mean?" If I get them appraised and they're worth a lot of money, do I give them back to her or does he take them?* It was a very strange situation.

But I kept thinking about it, and before I wore them, the pearl string broke. The necklace hadn't been worn in a while, but I could see that the pearls had been heavily used at one time because the string was worn almost through and one of the pearls was even damaged. They came from the jeweler Buccellati, so about a week after they broke I took them to Buccellati and asked to have them restrung and appraised for insurance purposes, because they had been given to me. Buccellati totally redid them. They restrung the strand

and even fixed the damaged pearl. The appraisal was for $14,500—but I did not say anything to Mr. Marshall about it; I waited for him to ask me. But he never did. I wondered whether he was he going to say, "Give them back to me." I sent Mrs. Astor a thank-you note. I decided that if Mr. Marshall asked me to give them back to her, I would give them back to Mrs. Astor directly. But I didn't trust him to take them from me himself—I had visions of him giving them to Charlene, not to Mrs. Astor. Anyway, he never said boo.

So now I wear these beautiful pearls, and I'll hand them down to a niece someday with a great story—that Mrs. Astor gave them to me with her own hand.

CHAPTER SIX

THE SEA CHANGE

As I said, Charlene was pleasant to me during my early years on the job, and I really thought we were friends. She was full of fun and unassuming, and we got along swimmingly. In fact, whenever she would call the office to speak to Mr. Marshall, she and I would chat and laugh for five minutes or so before I'd hand the phone to him and say, "Mr. Marshall, your wife wants to speak with you." But then things started to change, and I was mystified. I didn't know what was going on, but her attitude became different. I wasn't the only one who noticed. All Mrs. Astor's staff felt it.

The first time this happened was in 2002. It seemed a small thing at the time, but in retrospect it seems significant.

There was a mixup about some tickets that Mrs. Astor had purchased to a charity event—a fundraising dinner for either Save Venice or the Versailles Foundation; I forget which, but it had a "V" in it. Anyway, Mr. Marshall called me and said his mother had purchased four $1,000 tickets to the event, but she decided she wasn't going to go. He wanted to know if he could still use the tickets and take Charlene, her daughter, and her daughter's husband.

So I immediately called the organization and explained the situation, but they said that they had never gotten Mrs. Astor's check, and there was no reservation. (I thought this strange because I had a copy of the reservation in my file and a duplicate check for the four seats.) The check could have been lost in the mail. There had been a constant turnover of social secretaries since Jolee Hirsch left in 2001. No one had been with Mrs. Astor long enough to get the routine down pat, especially follow-up on Mrs. Astor's calendar. I made this inquiry to the organization the day before the event; even though it was so late, because this request was for Mrs. Astor's family, the organization said they would rearrange tables, etc... but they needed to know the names of those who were coming and whether they definitely would attend.

I called Mr. Marshall and told him all this, and he said, "Okay. I'll get back to you." A little while later he called me back and started asking me questions: Can you get the four seats? Do they need a check? Stuff like that. I explained that it could be done, but the organization needed the information right away. And so then I hear Mr. Marshall say to Charlene in the background, "Are we going to go? Stop see-sawing." And I heard Charlene say to him, "Well, it's Alice who's see-sawing." And I thought, *What is this all about?*

I still remember the incident because it was so vivid. I wondered what Charlene was talking about. I didn't have any say in the matter! If Charlene wanted the tickets, I could get them. She simply had to decide if she was going and give me the names of the people she was taking!

That was the first time I had any inkling that there was some kind of change in her. She was being a little nasty about me. I felt strange. I had never heard her talk that way about me, but I didn't say anything about it. I let it ride a while, but then her animosity toward me grew. It got worse. Several months later, she had made a complete turnaround—she didn't talk to *any* of us, none of the help. She went ballistic one day at 778 Park, at Mrs. Astor's apartment. I believe it was when Mrs. Astor was in Florida, but something had set off Charlene and she just started *screaming* at all the help. She was swearing and accusing them of taking advantage, doing this and that, it just went on and on. They all called me later. Mily was very resentful, and she spoke up to the Marshalls. They were all furious, but Charlene was on the warpath.

And then she simply stopped talking to Lourdes and me. She'd say hardly a word. Instead of chatting with me when she called, as she used to, she'd just say, "Is Tony there?" in a kind of angry voice. When I first heard this I thought, *Boy, she's not in a good mood. Something nasty must have happened.* And then I realized it was the way she was going to be to me. And she was never again in a good mood when she called.

Months went by, and finally I decided to ask Mr. Marshall about it. "Did I offend Mrs. Marshall," I asked. "Because she has started acting differently to me. If I've said or done anything to offend her, I'll apologize. I've been going over and over what it might have been, but I haven't come up with anything. Maybe I'm blind to it." But he just played dumb. There was no way he couldn't have known she was acting this way. He said he would try to find out, but he never got back to me on the subject.

I remember thinking that there was a subtle and now obvious change in dynamics. Mr. Marshall did not like dealing with the daily matters relating to Mrs. Astor. By early 2002, he was deferring more and more to Charlene, and she was becoming the dominant one. Perhaps his age (he was 77 by this time) was driving this in combination with Charlene possibly feeling more comfortable being in charge.

To this day I don't know for sure what caused her change in attitude from friendliness to brusqueness, but I think she just decided that "the help" was the help, and they were not going to be part of her life. She knew that we all were very loyal to Mrs. Astor, and Mrs. Astor and Charlene had only a chilly relationship. Now Charlene appeared to want to take over, and it soon became obvious that you were either in *her* court or you were in Mrs. Astor's court. She'd set up a dividing line.

Charlene must have felt overwhelmed when she first married Mr. Marshall and entered this new world of Mrs. Astor's, but by 2002, ten years after she had married Mr. Marshall, she had obviously started feeling her oats. By then she must have thought, *I'm Mrs. Marshall. I'm Brooke Astor's daughter-in-law, and I'm going to have some status here.* She started getting on the boards of New York institutions, theater production companies, the Advisory Committee of the Juilliard School of Music. (Although in every case it was Mrs. Astor who contributed the necessary money.) Anyway, her new demeanor was an eye-opener. Charlene's attitude just *spun around.*

There is one other reason that Charlene may have cooled to me, and the more I think about it the more likely it was the cause of her anger.

On December 28, 2001, I was at Mrs. Astor's apartment working on her jewelry, and Mrs. Astor was there preparing to go to Holly Hill for New Year's weekend. Raymonde and Mily and Lillian Sucur, another maid, were all buzzing around getting her ready, and she was sitting in her bedroom, chatting with me, looking very regal in a beautiful lace robe. She would be spending New Year's Eve with the Rockefellers, she told me. Suddenly, she had Raymonde bring out a gorgeous sable stole and said, "Try it on!!"

Well I did, and she looked at me and said, "That is beautiful, I think I'll keep it!!!" I laughed and said she should by all means. Then she told Raymonde to bring out the other fur neck piece which is also sable. I tried it on and she said, "Oh that's nice, why don't you take that?" My goodness, I was giddy! But then, she sent Raymonde to get her other stole, a black mink, and told me to try *that one* on. I did, and she declared that that stole suited me best and I should take that one and give Lourdes the sable neckpiece!

I protested but she was insistent. So I was sent off back to the office with a big shopping bag. Lourdes and I were overwhelmed with joy—more so because Mrs. Astor had given us these fabulous items that were hers. To us, they were better than new. I've worn the stole several times as a big fur collar over a coat, but I don't think Lourdes has ever worn her piece. She just looks at it—it's too precious to wear!

Now, Charlene very well could have felt that Lourdes and I should not have accepted the gifts (I'm not sure how you turn down Mrs. Astor). Both would have fitted Charlene, and she probably thought it was an insult to her that they were given to Lourdes and me. At the time, such a possible reaction didn't even cross my mind. But Charlene's coolness became noticeable to me sometime in early 2002. The timing is right for the fur-stole gift to have been the trigger for her change in attitude; that's the only thing that makes sense to me now.

How ironic that a fur piece might have caused this problem for me. John Jacob Astor started this entire mess by trapping furs!

In early 2003, it was a heady time for Charlene, particularly when she and her husband became involved in the theater world. It started out socially—through Whoopi Goldberg, of all people. When Whoopi and Frank Langella were a couple, they lived in the same apartment building as the Marshalls, and the two couples became friendly. They used to have dinner together occasionally, and the Marshalls always got invited to the big party Whoopi throws during the Holidays. There would be lots of celebrities and showbiz people there, and the Marshalls—both of them—seemed so excited about being in that milieu. I think it was through Langella that Mr. Marshall met the successful Broadway producer David Richenthal. Langella had starred in Richenthal's production of *Present Laughter,* and Richenthal had produced several Arthur Miller plays on Broadway. Now Mr. Marshall had been interested in the theater for a long time. As I've said, he had done a production of *Alice in Wonderland* years ago, but it was a flop. It opened in December of 1982 and closed after 21 performances.

When he met Richenthal, Mr. Marshall probably thought, *Gee, this could be a lot of fun. This guy is a major producer.* So they got together and they brought a revival of Eugene O'Neill's *Long Day's Journey Into Night* starring Vanessa Redgrave and Brian Dennehy to Broadway. As I mentioned, they wound up winning a Tony for it in 2003. As I recall, Mrs. Astor invested $100,000 in the play and recouped her investment, but she also personally contributed $25,000 for an opening-night party.

Soon after this hit, Mrs. Astor—or rather her money—was making increased theatrical investments. The first was a $250,000 payment to Barking Dog Productions, which was the company owned by David Richenthal. This money was going into an escrow account for future use. But it was the next two investments which caused me to lift my eyebrows. Now remember, Mr. Marshall was in charge of Mrs. Astor's investments; he controlled at least half of her money. So what did he do? He, Charlene, and Richenthal got together and formed Delphi Productions, and Mr. Marshall said to me, "Okay, I'm going to invest some of my mother's money." He had me write a check to Delphi for $250,000. Not long after, I was told to write another check for $250,000 to Delphi. So now Mrs. Astor had invested half a million dollars in this new production company, which, as everyone knows, is one of the riskiest investments on the planet. The

$500,000 bought ten shares in Delphi at $50,000 each and helped to bring *I Am My Own Wife* to Broadway. At some point, those shares were transferred to Mr. Marshall as a gift. Then, after *Wife*'s New York run, the producers wanted to take it to Chicago. So Mr. Marshall had me send a check for $200,000--again, of Mrs. Astor's money--as a "donation" to the Goodman Theater there, and that's how *I Am My Own Wife* got to Chicago. At least that money was tax-deductible.

Now none of that might sound *so* terrible, but events behind the scenes in those days just drove me crazy. Mrs. Astor's health had begun to decline in 2003, and I felt that the Marshalls really had started to take advantage of her. You've got to realize that before this decline set in, Mr. Marshall and Charlene were very deferential to Mrs. Astor—there was always, I assume, the thought that if you got on her bad side, she could pick up the phone, call her lawyer, and say, "I want to change my will"—who knows what she might do?

Mr. Marshall must have been a little afraid of her then, but things began to change when her health deteriorated. And once she broke her hip for the second time, in June 2003— that was disastrous for her—the Marshalls became very, very aggressive on the financial side. They stepped up in a *big* way and started changing everything.

Around March 2003 we started hiring nurses to look after Mrs. Astor, because everyone had become afraid of her falling.

. She was too independent for her own good at that point. In earlier years when she would come up to the office, especially if she had her dogs with her, I'd often say, "Mrs. Astor, would you like me to go down in the elevator with you?" And she'd say, "No, no." She didn't like to be babied, but we'd be nervous until we heard that she had made it safely.

However, by March 2003 we had private nurses at Mrs. Astor's apartment because of worry that she would get up in the middle of the night and fall with no one around to help her. In fact, Mily suggested that we put a gate at the top of the apartment stairs that led down to the fifteenth floor, just in case Mrs. Astor should take a tumble in the dark. Mily contacted a fellow who had worked in the apartment before and got an estimate for installing the gate-- $2,000. Everyone thought it would be a wise idea, but Mr. Marshall said "no." And that's something that always bothered me— why would he say no?

She was 101 at that time. She wore a hearing aid, and she was taking a lot of medication. I would get enormous bills for prescriptions every month. For years, Mrs. Astor had gotten her medications from Clayton and Edwards pharmacy. The bills came to thousands each month. I tried several times to explain that they could get the same medications from another pharmacy for a fraction of the cost as long as the pharmacy was in our medical plan, but it took a lot of convincing to change the old habits.

Mrs. Astor's doctor was Dr. Rees Pritchett at New York Hospital, and she visited him at least once a week, so I know he oversaw her health very carefully and closely. She had always tried to take good care of herself. For years she took B12 shots, and she would sometimes spend time at the spa at Baden-Baden in Germany. Everyone wanted to know what waters she was taking to have so much energy! Even though her health was declining--and soon was to drop precipitously--Mrs. Astor was still involved, still active, still engaged in the charitable work she had done for so many years.

Then something happened which I think was just unforgivable. In May 2003 Mrs. Astor went to a meeting at the Metropolitan Museum of Art—where she had been a mainstay for decades—and learned that the museum wanted to buy a Buddha for its collection. Another woman, Florence Irving, and Mrs. Astor immediately stepped forward and pledged the money to purchase the sculpture for the museum. Mrs. Astor's half of the contribution amounted to $117,000.

We got a letter from Philippe de Montebello, the elegant director of the museum, thanking Mrs. Astor for her gift— "You always come through for us. Thank you again..." But a few weeks later, on June 24, 2003, Mrs. Astor fell in her apartment and broke her hip for the second time. It was a bad break. She was in the hospital for a while, and had to return to the hospital in July for a second time to repair the damage.

And while she was in the hospital Mr. Marshall decided that he was not going to honor Mrs. Astor's pledge to the Metropolitan. He replied to de Montebello, saying that his mother didn't understand that she no longer could call on the resources of the Vincent Astor Foundation, which had finally closed in 2002, so she could not contribute to the purchase of the Buddha. Then he turned around and had me write that first check for $250,000—of Mrs. Astor's money—to Barking Dog Productions!

It just drove me *crazy*, I was so upset! On the one hand Mrs. Astor wanted to give $117,000 of her own money as a tax-deductible gift to the Metropolitan Museum, and her son said no, he was not sending it—I doubt he told her he was not sending her pledge—but he sent a $250,000 check to something he's involved in that *isn't* tax-deductible! I remember thinking, *This is not right. How can he do that? How can he justify this to himself?* He always used to try to justify his actions to me in some way, but saying Mrs. Astor couldn't make the donation because she didn't have the foundation anymore!? These were *her* funds. But now he was using them for *his* own purposes. I was livid. That was the beginning of my keeping notes on questionable things the Marshalls did. I was very concerned.

What I wanted to say to him was, "Mr. Marshall, how can you not pay the pledge that Mrs. Astor made? I don't understand." But I couldn't say anything. I just would have been immediately cut out. You know, sometimes I imagined he must have thought I was deaf, dumb, and blind. He would do or say something that was just so outrageous! Did he think I was stupid? But some powerful or privileged people get so used to their "help" being around that they don't think of them as human beings who are noticing what they are doing. He certainly seemed that way to me, because what appeared to be his mishandling of all that money was so blatant.

I've been asked why I didn't just quit and find a new job. Well, I felt that Mrs. Astor needed her long-term employees around her who knew the situation. New employees were conditioned to the Marshalls' needs, not Mrs. Astor's. And, on a personal level, I needed the health insurance. Today, the complexity of health insurance can control your life.

.

Anyway, Mrs. Astor came home from the hospital, but she soon had to go back for more work on her broken hip, and I went to visit her. I took a little orchid for her, but when I walked into her room at New York Hospital I felt a little embarrassed—the room was bulging with huge baskets of beautiful flowers. Chris Ely, her devoted butler from Holly Hill, was there when I arrived. I didn't stay very long, but her doctor came in while I was there. I remember the doctor's saying something about hoping to see Mrs. Astor in Maine that summer-- meaning he thought she might still go--but that wasn't to be. Mr. Marshall and Charlene were already up at Cove End, while Mrs. Astor would spend the summer recuperating at Holly Hill.

Mrs. Astor was in decent shape while in the hospital, but you could tell her old sparkle was going. She was still aware of everything around her, and she eventually recovered enough to be able to walk...but no more sparkle. Her health was crumbling. She would never be the same again. So my visit was a sad one. While there, I heard from Chris, who went to the hospital every day to sit with Mrs. Astor, that Annette de la Renta, who was like a daughter to Mrs. Astor, had been to visit at the hospital and confided to him the story about Mrs. Astor's $117,000 pledge to the Metropolitan to purchase the Buddha. Mr. Marshall refused to honor his mother's pledge, and the Museum had to find another source to cover the cost. I could just imagine the chatter at the museum about what was going on.

When Mrs. Astor made the pledge, she couldn't have known what soon would happen to her—her broken hip and declining health. She couldn't have known that would be the last meeting she would attend at the Metropolitan, the last time, in fact, she would be an active part of that great world. I'm sure she never knew that her son had refused to honor her pledge. Had she known, I think she would have been so *mortified.*

In the end, according to Philippe de Montebello's later testimony at the Anthony Marshall trial in 2009, Mrs. Astor's portion of the cost of the Buddha was paid for with money from an existing Astor fund for Asian Art. Today, one can view this *Seated Buddha with Double Lotus Base* in the Asian Art section of the Museum. It is Burmese, from the late eleventh century.

⊸∞∞∞⊸

CHAPTER SEVEN

THE DRAMA

Mrs. Astor's breaking her hip for the second time, in June 2003, seemed to me to signal to the Marshalls that they'd better make some moves to secure as much of her money as they could for themselves. Every day some new outrage was perpetrated. This was the beginning of a disturbing time for Mrs. Astor and for those who worked for her, loved her and were devoted to her.

The Marshalls were supposed to leave for London to attend Wimbledon the day after Mrs. Astor's fall. Understandably, they were very disappointed to have to cancel their trip. I sympathized--until I had to take the brunt of Mr. Marshall's frustration. He lashed out at me for something I'd nothing to do with. Later, he apologized. But, all the same, this was a definite turning point—it was no longer business as usual at the Astor office.

There had already been warning signs, certain transactions that just didn't make sense to me—and one of the first was that sale in early 2002 of Mrs. Astor's beloved painting by American Impressionist Childe Hassam, *Flags, Fifth Avenue*. This is a colorful, exuberant work that Hassam had painted in 1917 after viewing the Preparedness Day parade in New York in May 1916, one of the first large demonstrations in support of U.S. intervention in World War I. Hassam had given the painting, one of a series of influential "flag" paintings he completed, to the Art Students League of New York. Mrs. Astor bought it in 1970 for $167,000 from the Wildenstein Gallery and hung it, as I've mentioned, in pride of place over the fireplace in the library of her New York apartment. She loved that painting, not for its monetary value but for its vibrancy, its patriotism, its sheer color and enthusiasm.

After September 11, 2001, you may well imagine how much more important—and valuable-- the painting had become. For people who had lived in New York in the months after 9/11, Hassam's 84-year-old work of art had taken on the air of a historic documentary! Every New York street and avenue blossomed with American flags—just like Hassam's painting did.

In that frantic period--in late 2001 or early 2002--Mr. Marshall decided to sell the painting. How he persuaded

Mrs. Astor to part with it I'll never know. He always used to warn her that she was spending too much money, and maybe he convinced her that selling the Childe Hassam was a financial necessity. Mr. Marshall had found a dealer who was willing to pay $10 million for it, and he claimed that that was a good offer. He told me that he would take a 15 percent commission on the sale. (I later found out he took 20 percent.) So he sold the painting for $10 million to Gerald Peters, an art dealer in Santa Fe.

Was it a good deal? Well, it definitely was for Gerald Peters. Not too long after buying the painting, he resold it to a private collector, reportedly for more than $20 million. So he made some $10 million by taking advantage of Mr. Marshall's naiveté about the art market. And it was still a good deal for Mr. Marshall, who took a $2 million commission as Mrs. Astor's agent. But the loser here, obviously, was Mrs. Astor—and also the city of New York. Prior to 2002, Mrs. Astor's will had stipulated that after her death the painting was to go to the Metropolitan Museum of Art, as long as the museum would put it on display as part of its permanent collection. Now that may never happen.

My own feelings were that there was absolutely no reason to sell the painting. Mrs. Astor did not need the money. The painting reminded me of a wonderful couple of hours I spent lunching with Mrs. Astor at her apartment--just the two of us, seated at a small table set up in her library, with me facing the Childe Hassam. I can recall many details of the experience. Boysie, Mrs. Astor's dachshund, jumped into my lap and remained there throughout the entire lunch. Mrs. Astor told me the story, which I have mentioned, of the time she was lost in the dark at Hatfield House. She asked me to help her after lunch to fax a note to Prince Charles on his 50th birthday. Her secretary was away for the day, so she wrote out a birthday greeting, signed it "your ancient friend," and asked me to please fax it for her. We rode down on the elevator together from her apartment; she was off to an appointment and I walked cheerily back to the office. What a divine day for me! It was Friday, November 13, 1998.

With the money he'd made from selling the Childe Hassam, Mr. Marshall bought, a few months after the sale, a relatively modest country house in Bernardsville, New Jersey, a tony New York City suburb. I thought this was strange because that's where his unloving biological father, Dryden Kuser, used to live. Mr. Marshall had been born in that town. And something else seemed odd. Mr. Marshall asked me to please not tell anyone-- especially his mother-- that he had this house in New Jersey. He said she would not understand why he wanted a house in New Jersey. I assumed he wanted his privacy; that desire was fine with me, but in the back of my head I was thinking, *If his mother finds out he bought a house in New Jersey, she's going to know that's why he wanted to sell the painting and take a commission.* I honored his request. Whenever he asked me to keep quiet, I did—but I didn't forget.

And there is a postscript to the *Flags* story. Mr. Marshall claimed on Mrs. Astor's tax return that Mrs. Astor had paid $5 million for the Childe Hassam, but the actual price had only been $167,000. When this discrepancy was discovered by JPMorgan Chase in 2006, Mr. Marshall immediately re-filed the tax return, and he told the IRS that this was just a bookkeeping mistake.

Also, in the spring of 2003, Mr. Marshall fired Mrs. Astor's social secretary, Naomi Packard Dunn, a tall, attractive, young woman with a Princeton degree, whom he had hired the year before and about whom he had spoken glowingly to me—until she showed too much concern for Mrs. Astor. What I learned was that Mrs. Astor was hosting a dinner party for eight people at her apartment in honor of Kofi Annan. Mr. Marshall took it upon himself to add four more to the guest list, including Mike Wallace and his wife. Naomi pointed out to him that Mrs. Astor had trouble hearing when there were so many people. So wouldn't it be better to keep the guest list to eight, as Mrs. Astor intended?

That questioning of his wishes was the beginning of the end for Naomi. The Marshalls were demanding that the staff be loyal primarily to them. So they fired Naomi and hired a young woman, Erica Meyer, who was a friend of Mrs. Marshall's daughter, as Mrs. Astor's new social secretary. We other employees assumed she was a "spy" for the Marshalls which put this nice young woman in a very awkward position. She was paid by Mrs. Astor, but many of her responsibilities were for the Marshalls' new production company, Delphi. Like the rest of us, she did what she was told to do, but a little more than two years after she was hired, the honeymoon with the Marshalls was over: She was dismissed, rather cruelly, in September 2005, just after her return from her honeymoon!

When I came on board in November of 1993, I soon learned that Mrs. Astor owned the apartment at 79th Street and Lexington Avenue where the Marshalls lived. It was a substantial two-bedroom apartment in a prestigious building. Then, around 1996, the Marshalls became eager to acquire the two-room apartment directly below theirs, which had just come on the market. Mrs. Astor bought the apartment, and a huge renovation was planned so that the two floors could be connected. The renovation took a long time. The Marshalls lived in the guest house at Holly Hill while the work went on. When they got back home, they had a stunning duplex apartment, compliments of Mrs. Astor.

Not long after the completion of the renovation, the ownership of the duplex was turned over to Mr. Marshall, who then turned it over to Charlene. But Mrs. Astor continued to pay for all the couple's fixed living expenses—the monthly maintenance, the garage fees, telephones, electricity, insurance, Mr. Marshall's dental expenses, etc. I remember that one time the Marshalls replaced the windows in the apartment, and Mr. Marshall had me write him a check, telling me his mother wanted to give him the new windows as a birthday gift.

Similarly, even after Mrs. Astor gave Cove End to Mr. Marshall in early 2003, and he turned it over to Charlene later in the year, Mrs. Astor continued to pay all the expenses there too--heating fuel, electricity, telephones, cable, maintenance. I'd even get bills for their groceries!

Mrs. Astor also paid the salaries of the three gardeners, the housekeeper, and even two women—a cook and a maid— whom the Marshalls brought up from Antigua to work for them for the summer. That summer of 2004, Mr. Marshall transferred $10,000 from Mrs. Astor's account to the Marshalls' bank account in Maine, and then paid $500 cash a week to each woman for ten weeks. Mrs. Astor also paid for the Antiguans' plane fares and uniforms.

I was under the impression that at that time (2004), one could legally give away only $11,000 a year tax free to each of one's children. I thought how amazing it was that many, many thousands of dollars went annually to Mr. Marshall that weren't counted as either income or gift. Was this allowed by law? So I had to assume he knew what loopholes existed—but I didn't think it was right, ethically speaking. But what did I know? I was so concerned, however, that I eventually called Mrs. Astor's accountant, Steve Cohen, and asked him if I was in any way accountable for writing these checks. He said, "Well, Mrs. Astor still uses Cove End, doesn't she?" And I said, "No, she hasn't been there since the summer of 2002." Then he asked me if I signed the checks, and I told him no. So he said I was not liable in any way. But I could tell from the hesitation in his voice that he had been under the impression that even though Cove End was no longer in Mrs. Astor's name, she was still using it and, therefore, could pay all the household bills.

The staff used to joke around sometimes, trying to figure out what Mr. Marshall did with his salary, which was several hundred thousand dollars a year. Since all his expenses were paid by his mother, where did he spend his salary? Did he just hoard it? It was a puzzlement!

After Mrs. Astor broke her hip so disastrously, the "gifts" became more dramatic—and more questionable. Now, remember, this is early August 2003; at this point Mrs. Astor is 101 and she is recuperating at Holly Hill. I was told by Chris Ely that she had met with her lawyer, Henry ("Terry") Christensen, of Sullivan & Cromwell on August 13. The result of that meeting was that Mrs. Astor signed a letter addressed to Mr. Marshall stating that she wanted to give Mr. Marshall $5 million outright so that he could provide for Charlene's future, and Mr. Christensen delivered the letter to Mr. Marshall. (I gained access to that letter during the court case.) I found this most peculiar. Mrs. Astor had just gotten out of the hospital after breaking her hip, and did it make sense that Charlene was what she would be thinking about?

Around this same time, August 2003, I started getting suspicious that something improper was going on with the Vincent Astor Trust – the main source of Mrs. Astor's income. She had stipulated in her will where this money was to go when she died. Its $60 million were earmarked for her favorite charities. Mr. Marshall had no control of this trust, but Richard Thieke, a trust officer at Bankers Trust (now Deutsche Bank), who did, would meet once or twice a year with Mr. Marshall for lunch and update him on the operations of the trust. After all, Mr. Marshall was Mrs. Astor's financial manager, so it was important that he be kept informed.

One day, I noted that Mr. Marshall had written a letter to Mr. Thieke about their meeting at Bankers Trust, thanking him profusely for his friendship and for being so helpful. *Hmmmm….why would the meeting be at this man's office and what was he thanking him for?* I could only conclude one thing: Some money in the trust was in some way being rerouted so that when Mrs. Astor died, Mr. Marshall would have control of where it would go. I had no proof of this, but I felt sure I was on the right track. Now how could Mr. Marshall have orchestrated this? At the time, I hadn't a clue.

Then in early February 2004, Mr. Marshall fired Mrs. Astor's longtime lawyer, Mr. Christensen. I was listening to Mr.

Marshall speak on the phone to him in a cordial and friendly tone. When he hung up, he came out of his office and said to me, "I feel terrible. Terry is getting a letter on Monday telling him he is no longer Mrs. Astor's lawyer, power of attorney, or executor." I was shocked. Why would Mr. Marshall be firing Terry Christensen? I suspected that Mr. Marshall must have asked Terry to do something involving the will, but that Terry had refused. But, I thought, Mr. Christensen would vehemently fight this dismissal.

A few weeks later, Mr. Marshall told me that Terry hadn't been working in Mrs. Astor's best interest, and that Terry had come to see the Marshalls at their apartment and threatened Mr. Marshall. I thought to myself, *What could he be threatening him with?* Now the wheels were really turning in my head, and I wondered what Mr. Christensen would do. I speculated that he certainly would fight to stay on board--but maybe he had compromised his position in some way.

Meanwhile, Mr. Marshall had hired Francis X. Morrissey, Jr., a Park Avenue attorney and a friend of his and Charlene's, and Warren Whitaker of the law firm Day, Berry and Howard, as Mrs. Astor's new lawyers. And they recommended he hire a litigator, Kenneth Warner, to deal with Terry Christensen, who was refusing to turn over the will and other documents that they needed. I had no proof, again, but I knew something was fishy.

Mr. Marshall had also told me after he fired Mr. Christensen that the new lawyers were abolishing the trust that Mrs. Astor planned to leave him in her will for him to live off of (as Vincent had done for Mrs. Astor), and instead she was giving her money to Mr. Marshall outright when she died so he could then leave it to Charlene. This seemed improper to me since I knew Mrs. Astor was not a big fan of her daughter-in-law, and she had recently given that $5 million to Mr. Marshall to take care of Charlene. Mrs. Astor had stated unequivocally in her will that the trust she was leaving to "Tony" was to go to charity when Mr. Marshall died, not to Charlene and her three children. Mrs. Astor's wishes were being totally disregarded. Charlene was now being positioned to inherit most of the Astor money. I was feeling really queasy about all this.

Shortly thereafter, I started getting bills from all the new lawyers and they pretty much spelled out what was going on: codicils to Mrs. Astor's will, estate planning, establishment of the Anthony D. Marshall Foundation, handling of the Terry Christensen situation, etc. I knew now that Mrs. Astor's will and legacy were being changed but how was this being done?

After her fall in June 2003, I knew through the conversations between all her employees, that Mrs. Astor could not clearly understand complex financial matters. Were Mr. Marshall and these new lawyers having her sign things that she could not understand? Would a 101-year-old woman suddenly decide to make such major changes to her will? I had a lot of questions, and I felt very uncomfortable with what I saw happening. But to whom could I talk? Mr. Marshall was Mrs. Astor's only child, and I had no idea at that time where Mr. Marshall's two sons stood on such family matters.

Also, in 2003, as I have mentioned, Mr. and Mrs. Marshall got totally involved in their theatre productions, and that's where Mr. Marshall was concentrating his energies and investing some of Mrs. Astor's money. Mr. Marshall would come into the office for 10 minutes a day, if at all, and only to sign checks--I did not have check signing authority, thank goodness--and to pick up his mail. I felt that the office was now just a burden to him, and he really didn't have time for it. Luckily for him, Lourdes and I could handle everything, and did. I often thought at the time that Mr. Marshall felt that we were just necessary evils that he had to contend with—as little as possible.

One funny note: Mr. Marshall had told me, when he first started working on *Long Day's Journey,* that I would of course get tickets. I am still waiting. And when *I Am My Own Wife* opened, he handed me a flyer offering discounted tickets for a performance. I'm still flabbergasted. At that point I had worked for the man for more than 10 years, and he wanted me to buy tickets to his play! The fact that he had me

photocopy 12 copies of a 50-page contract for the play should
have at least landed me a ticket or two, don't you think?

So when Philip Marshall filed the petition with the court in
July 2006, I finally got to see the papers which would con-
firm everything that I had suspected. These papers were correspondence between lawyers, wills from 1997, 2001, 2002,
and three codicils. The story went like this:

At the end of 2003, Mr. Christensen was involved with Mr.
Marshall in adding the first codicil to Mrs. Astor's will.
Sullivan & Cromwell, the very old-line New York law firm,
had represented Mrs. Astor for 40 years. Christensen was her
lawyer there, her co-power of attorney with Mr. Marshall,
and the co-executor of her will.

For years, I used to hear that Mrs. Astor frequently changed
her will. She was always having Christensen come up to her
apartment, but nobody knew what was in the document.
Mr. Marshall once said to me, "I don't know what's in my
mother's will." At some point, he must have gotten to take
a peek.

Mr. Christensen apparently agreed to some changes in the
will that Mr. Marshall asked for, and the first codicil changed
the disposition of the Vincent Astor Trust after Mrs. Astor's
death. (As I had suspected!) Mrs. Astor's will had direct-
ed that the Vincent Astor Trust money go to her favorite

charities after her death. The first codicil, which Christensen oversaw, said that now Mr. Marshall would have a say in where 49 percent of the money would go. Mr. Marshall then started his own foundation—the Anthony D. Marshall Foundation—and Charlene started one too—the Shepherd Community Foundation. I understood that to mean that 49 percent of the trust would now go to *their* foundations for them to oversee. Charlene would become the new Mrs. Astor! Without the name, of course.

My guess is Mr. Christensen must have felt pressured to write that codicil, and probably thought, *Well, this isn't a terrible thing. The money is still going to charity.* Obviously, I did not know what he was thinking, but it was the only thing that made sense to me.

Two months later, Mr. Marshall fired him. Terry had been asked to write a second codicil that would abolish the trust Mrs. Astor was setting up for Mr. Marshall to live off of after her death, and would instead give him the money outright so he could leave it to Charlene. Mr. Christensen protested to Mr. Marshall that Mrs. Astor was not competent to sign the second codicil. Yet only two months before, he had let her sign the first codicil—and he hadn't seen her during those two months. The second codicil would change the very essence of Mrs. Astor's will and Terry obviously felt that, as her lawyer, he could not do that. But he had written the first codicil and that's what compromised his position (as I suspected!) What a tangled web. A copy of a letter I received from Philip written by Mr. Whitaker, the new lawyer, and sent to Mr. Christensen, confirmed my suspicion.

Now Mr. Marshall had become the *sole* power-of-attorney for his mother, and the co-executors of Mrs. Astor's will would now become Charlene and her pal, the lawyer Francis Morrissey, the same guy who years before had been accused of defrauding several elderly clients--cases that were settled with no admission of guilt.

Then a third codicil also was signed in 2004, and that's the one that really raised red flags. It was meant to minimize estate taxes, but it was Mrs. Astor's signature that was controversial. By that time her handwriting had become very shaky and spidery, but the signature on this codicil is strongly written—much as she would have signed things a long time ago. So the question arose—was her signature forged? I didn't know, but I questioned why she signed any of the codicils.

It all came down to Mrs. Astor's competency, and that's another tangled web. Going back a number of years--around 2001—Mr. Marshall said to me that Mrs. Astor had been diagnosed with Alzheimer's disease in late 2000. I thought to myself, "Wow!" because I hadn't noticed it, but I didn't see her all the time. He told me that there were…indications… and that a doctor had confirmed that she did indeed have Alzheimer's. Mr. Marshall told me not to tell anybody, of course—not to talk about it, which I never did. I'm good at keeping secrets.

But then one day, in late 2001, one of the maids called the office and said Mrs. Astor had Alzheimer's. After that, we'd talk about it among ourselves, but we *never* mentioned it to anyone else. Part of me thought, *Hmmmm, maybe Mr. Marshall is just saying that so he can take over making more of the decisions.*

Well, silly me. Sometime later, there was a whole retraction of the Alzheimer's story. I don't recall Mr. Marshall saying it to me, but the word around the office was, "Oh, no, she doesn't *really* have Alzheimer's." *How can that be?* I was sure the courts were going to be looking into all that. Because if she had Alzheimer's in 2000, what was she doing changing her will in 2003? And 2004? Can a person with Alzheimer's change her will? Can she sign legal documents?

So, Mrs. Astor was said to have signed all three codicils. I noticed that many of the legal bills were addressed to her as though the lawyers had discussed all their contents with her in detail. And in February 2004, there was a luncheon at the Knickerbocker Club at which Mrs. Astor read to her guests (the Marshalls, Francis Morrissey, Richard Thieke, Freddy Melhado who was a friend of Mrs. Astor's and an investor of some of her money, and Dr. Pritchett) a proclamation saying how much she appreciated everything her son did for her and how much she loved him and his wife. The luncheon was paid for by Francis Morrissey, also a member of the Knickerbocker, but then charged back as a disbursement on one of his bills to Mrs. Astor. That seemed strange to me, because if Mrs. Astor was hosting the luncheon and she was a member of the Knickerbocker Club, why didn't they just charge her account? My sense of it all was that she never initiated the luncheon or wrote the words that she spoke at it. I think the entire event was staged. After that, Mrs. Astor never wanted to go back to the Knickerbocker Club. She had been traumatized.

Throughout 2004, I watched Mr. Marshall prepare for the demise of his mother and for his own future. He opened a revocable trust in his mother's name that appointed himself as its trustee, and he took a fee for overseeing it. The trust would pay Mrs. Astor's bills after she died and before the will was probated. He fired Alicia Johnson, who had been Mrs. Astor's housekeeper for twelve years in Maine, and hired someone new for Cove End now that the Marshalls owned it.

He stopped sending money to many of Mrs. Astor's favorite charities, explaining to me that he wasn't giving to organizations that his mother wasn't getting pleasure from anymore, such as The Frick Collection. My routine was to present him with requests for personal contributions that came in the mail. I would write on the request the amount Mrs. Astor had given the prior year, and Mr. Marshall would return the request to me with an answer. At this point, most of his answers were "take no action." Yet he would send contributions from Mrs. Astor to organizations with which the Marshalls were involved. They were very active at the American Museum of Natural History, so there were still contributions sent to that venerable institution. At one point during the summer, he called me from Maine and told me that Erica Meyer, then Mrs. Astor's social secretary, would be working for Delphi, his production company, but still out of Mrs. Astor's apartment.

Late in 2004, Mr. Marshall took one of the two Tiepolo paintings that hung on either side of the fireplace in the living room at 778. He said Mrs. Astor had given it to him as a Christmas gift and asked me to take it off the insurance. I did. He also deleted several of the people that were on Mrs. Astor's Christmas gift list, but increased the amounts given to those people who worked for him.

On January 7, 2005, Mr. Marshall shut down Holly Hill, saying Mrs. Astor should stay closer to her doctors, and going back and forth weekends was not good for her. I think he was especially pleased to get rid of Chris Ely, the butler, who was very close to Mrs. Astor. I believe that's why he shut down Holly Hill. It was the only way he could fire Chris without starting trouble. He kept on the three gardeners and the round-the-clock security.

As spring rolled around, it looked like Mrs. Astor, for the first time in her life, was going to spend the summer cooped up in her apartment. We all thought that that was a bad idea and I was thrilled when I got a call from Annette de la Renta wanting to set up a meeting with David Rockefeller and Tony at Mr. Rockefeller's office. The result of the meeting was that Mrs. Astor would return to Holly Hill for the summer of '05. What a collective sigh of relief! Evidently, Mr. Rockefeller and Mrs. de la Renta "leaned" on Mr. Marshall to move his mother to Holly Hill for the summer. I heard later that Mr. Rockefeller said he would take Mrs. Astor to his home in Maine if Tony didn't open Holly Hill. That must have convinced Tony that it would be embarrassing if Mrs. Astor was in Maine but not at Cove End. So preparations were made to reopen Holly Hill. The covers were taken off the furniture, the house was cleaned and aired out, and Mrs. Astor returned to Holly Hill with her nurses and household help from the city. On June 15, 2005, the Marshalls got on a new boat they had purchased and made their way up the coast to Cove End for the summer. I recall that they did not come down even one time that summer to visit Mrs. Astor.

CHAPTER EIGHT

FIRINGS AND FILINGS

I've mentioned Mr. Marshall's thriftyness before, but most of the staff saw it up-close- and-personal when he started to lay off employees. I don't know whether all of the others were aware of his tight-fistedness before they got fired, but I had seen it on so many occasions I lost count. Let me give you a few examples:

One time Francis Morrissey, before he became Mrs. Astor's lawyer, came up to the office for lunch. Mr. Marshall brought up a couple of sandwiches and two bags of potato chips from Pret A Manger, and I put them on plates for them. They had a closed-door meeting in Mr. Marshall's office. When the lunch ended and Mr. Morrissey left, Mr. Marshall came out of his office and asked me to put the leftover chips back in the bag so he could take them home. I had to fish the bag out of the trash! I mean, come on—Lourdes and I could have eaten the chips or I could just have thrown them out! Extreme thriftiness? I guess you could call it that.

Then during one holiday season, the building management dropped off a basket of goodies for our office. Lourdes was on vacation, and I put the basket on the files behind my desk. When Mr. Marshall came in he asked where the basket was from. I told him, and he went over, took off the cellophane wrapper, and divided the goodies into separate piles for the three of us. I felt like saying, "Why don't you just take the whole basket home with you," but of course I didn't. I thought it would have been nice to leave the basket there for all of us to share everything, but...no. He took the items he liked home. What did he need with more food?

Speaking of the holidays, after the Astor Foundation closed we no longer had the cozy little Christmas parties that we had enjoyed every year. Instead, Mr. Marshall would bring a little gift for Lourdes and me, and that was it. So one Christmas he brought us each our gifts and after he left, we opened them. I got a colorful little ceramic pitcher and Lourdes received a little china elephant by Lynn Chase, who designs all sorts of wild animal china. I knew the Marshalls went each year to a Lynn Chase showroom sale, and I assume that's where they picked up this little elephant. However, I noticed that the elephant was one half of a set of salt-and-pepper shakers.

And the cork stopper that was supposed to hold in the salt or pepper was missing. I don't know whether Mr. Marshall realized what he had done, but he should have. To me, this was an insult to faithful, reliable, uncomplaining Lourdes, who had worked for him for almost 20 years at the time. I felt so badly for her. I mean, what do you write in a thank-you note? Thank you for the defective saltshaker? I have always wondered whether he knew what it was and didn't care, or hadn't even looked closely enough to realize it was defective.

Another time I got a call from my very dear friend Linda Sage, telling me that Montefiore hospital had honored Mrs. Astor some 30 years before, and they were having another fundraiser and wanted Mrs. Astor to be the honoree again. Could I help them out? Well, at that point Mrs. Astor was in her late nineties, and I told my friend it was doubtful that she would be able to attend the function—but, I said, if my friend would send a letter about the proposal, I would make sure that Mr. Marshall would read it.

Now, understand that requests for this sort of thing came in on a regular basis, and Mrs. Astor would decline but always send a check for $100, $200, $500—something. So I was pretty sure that Mr. Marshall would decline but tell me to send a little check to the hospital for their fundraiser. Instead, he returned my friend's letter to me with a note saying, "It's a worthy cause, but not possible at this time." I was more than astounded! I had two thoughts: One, if he valued me as a loyal assistant who had never asked for a donation to anything, wouldn't he show his appreciation with even a small gift to the hospital? And two, maybe he didn't want to start a precedent that would encourage me to ask for other gifts. Well, the former seemed anyone's normal response. The latter lumped me in with everyone else who came to Mrs. Astor for donations—just someone else who was after his mother's money. I was highly insulted—and embarrassed that I had to go back empty-handed to my friend.

There was another incident involving a friend that I found very revealing about Mr. Marshall's character. This friend is a businessman who has factories in China, does a lot of business there, and knows many of the country's politicians and major officials. Through his connections he had heard that the new Chinese ambassador, the Consul-General in New York, was miffed because Mayor Giuliani had never invited him to Gracie Mansion or made any attempt to meet him. My friend didn't know anyone on the Mayor's staff that he could tell about this, but he had the idea that perhaps Mrs. Astor could arrange an event where Mayor Giuliani and the Chinese Ambassador might meet. He knew that Mrs. Astor had spent several childhood years in China and had a long-standing love of the country. Perhaps she could invite both to one of her famous dinners at her apartment.

Well, I wouldn't go over Mr. Marshall's head and take this directly to Mrs. Astor, so I brought it up with Mr. Marshall.

I had never asked him to do anything personally for me. I never felt he would welcome it, and I didn't want to put him in an awkward position, but this was a fascinating situation and I thought it might interest him.

So I told him the whole story. He sat back in his chair and thought about it. First he mentioned that perhaps he'd talk to Philippe de Montebello about getting Giuliani and the ambassador together at some event at the Metropolitan Museum of Art. Then he started musing and thinking out loud. "How can I benefit from this?" he said, and I was stunned. Stunned! I said nothing, of course, but I was think-ing, *This isn't about you*! Either he would be doing a favor for me, at the very least, or, at best, doing a favor for New York City and its relations with China! But that is how Mr. Marshall's mind worked. He was so self-absorbed that all he could think of was how this situation could help *him* in some way. Needless to say, nothing ever came of it.

So it was in the context of this behavior that I worried about what would become of all of us when Mrs. Astor died. None of Mrs. Astor's employees had a retirement plan. Lourdes and I had brought up the question several times over the last few years of our employment, but Mr. Marshall did not want to address the issue. We asked what would happen to the office when Mrs. Astor died, and he inferred that it would take a while to settle the estate and he would need help. But there was no specific plan. At our last attempt to discuss a retirement fund with him he said he'd think about it. I guess he's still thinking! My fear was that Mr. Marshall would give as little as he could get away with—because it would take away from his own inheritance.

One of the most uncomfortable parts of my job was to talk to staffers who had been fired about their health insurance options. I was in charge of the insurance, so it was my responsibility. When employees lost their jobs, they also lost their health insurance, and by law I had to offer them COBRA— which allowed them to stay on the insurance for 18 months. Of course, the person has to pay for COBRA, and the premiums are exorbitant!! So that was a very painful thing for me to do, but I had that discussion with everyone who was let go. Most could not afford the insurance.

In May of 2004, when Mr. Marshall told Alicia Johnson, who had been Mrs. Astor's Maine housekeeper for 12 years, that she was being dismissed, he told her they weren't going to hire anyone to take her place. He offered her $5,000 severance, but said that she shouldn't apply for unemployment. How dare he? She was entitled to it! When the separation day came, Alicia said that she had heard the Marshalls had indeed hired someone to replace her—so Mr. Marshall gave her $10,000. (Alicia had heard right. The Marshalls hired Anna Silver as housekeeper at Cove End, I believe on the recommendation of Martha Stewart, the famous lifestyle guru, who had a home nearby.) There also were four gardeners at

Cove End. Three of them, the Hamors, were a father and two sons who had worked for Mrs. Astor for years and years. Steve Hamor, Sr., the father and head groundskeeper, was told by Mr. Marshall to inform the fourth gardener, Tim Sheehan, who had worked there for ten years, that he was being let go in a month. The man was so upset he just walked off then and there. Mr. Marshall never sent him any severance money.

In January 2005, Mr. Marshall turned his attention to Holly Hill, Mrs. Astor's beloved retreat in Westchester County, and its staff. One day he drove up there with Charlene, their lawyer Francis Morrissey, and Erica Meyer, Mrs. Astor's supposed social secretary, who actually worked for their theater company, Delphi Productions. I think Mr. Marshall wanted some backup for his mission. He told the butler and estate manager Chris Ely that they were closing Holly Hill and, therefore, letting him go. Mr. Marshall said that his mother was too frail to visit Holly Hill anymore, she should stay closer to her doctors in New York City, and it didn't make sense to keep the country house open.

Again, I believe the real reason for closing Holly Hill was that Mr. Marshall wanted to get rid of Chris Ely. A man of about forty at the time with proper English manners, Chris could be tough, but he got the job done. He ran a tight ship at Holly Hill, and he was fiercely devoted to Mrs. Astor, making sure the house was run to her standards, driving her wherever she wanted to go in the country, and protecting her time and energies. He and the Marshalls disliked each other, though they remained outwardly cordial. The story is, one of the cooks at the apartment who did not get along with Chris sent a letter to the Marshalls telling them that Chris made negative comments about Mrs. Marshall. A copy of this letter had come across my desk at one point.

Chris told me that Mr. Marshall offered him a month's pay as severance--which was a pittance--but Mr. Marshall said Chris was in Mrs. Astor's will and would get more when she died. Chris didn't say anything. He didn't balk or ask for more severance; he didn't do anything. But he was livid. In his quiet way, he let the rest of the staff know that it wasn't over yet.

Holly Hill was shuttered. They took out all the phones except one, they turned off the cable TV, they turned down the thermostat to 55 degrees, and had all the furniture covered. (We later learned that several valuable paintings were removed from the house about this time, but eventually they were returned by court order.) The only staffers kept on were the gardeners and security people. Chris moved out, found a place to live in Westchester, and began working as a butler on a freelance basis. I think he worked a while for the Rockefellers, and then he commuted to Washington to work for some people down there.

But he continued to stay in touch with Mrs. Astor. In fact, he somehow managed to visit her once a week in her New

York apartment. When Mr. Marshall found out about that, he immediately put a stop to it—Chris was barred from seeing her again. In fact, Mr. Marshall drew up a list of people who would be allowed to see his mother. It was a very short list. In my opinion, that only caused her to decline more rapidly—she was getting no stimulation, receiving few visitors from the outside world in which she always had been so active.

Now, Erica Meyer had been hired as Mrs. Astor's social secretary in 2003 after Naomi Dunn was let go. As I said, she was a friend of one of Charlene Marshall's daughters, and when she first was hired we all suspected that she was a "spy" for the Marshalls. That suspicion turned out to be very unfair to Erica, who was a very sweet young woman thrown into something way over her head. She really thought that she was being hired as Mrs. Astor's social secretary, but it quickly became obvious that she was supposed to work for Delphi Productions—and the producer David Richenthal, who had been given an office in Mrs. Astor's apartment. The Marshalls were totally involved in their theater company at the time, and in early 2005 they had gone over to London to put on a production of *Death of a Salesman.* Erica went with them, but apparently something backfired. I don't know the whole story, but after that, the Marshalls were sour on Erica.

So I was having a phone conversation with Erica in June 2005 and she mentioned that the Marshalls were acting strangely toward her. Their attitude had changed, but she didn't know why. She was busy with plans for her own wedding, which took place late that summer. The very day she returned from her honeymoon, the Marshalls were awaiting her arrival at Mrs. Astor's apartment, and they told her she was being dismissed then and there. Erica was devastated. She was crying to Mily. But she was locked out, and that was the end of that. I'm sure she put all this behind her and got on with her life, but I think it was a harsh reality for her at the time. I tried calling her to commiserate with her about being fired, but she never called me back. She didn't want to talk to me or, later, to Philip (or even to the investigators after the petition had been filed with the court). about her experience, but I know the court got in touch with her and she had to testify at Mr. Marshall's trial. For one thing, she was in Mrs. Astor's apartment during the time the lawyers were going up there and having Mrs. Astor sign the codicils to the will. But after she got fired she wanted nothing to do with any of it, and I can't blame her.

What happened to Marciano Amaral is another story. Marciano had become more than Mrs. Astor's chauffeur during the 10 years he worked for her—he was her confidante and trusted companion, walking her dogs, doing errands, and just being there whenever she wanted to talk. He was a good listener and she felt secure with him. Marciano had owned a restaurant in his native Portugal, and he's also a talented sculptor, an art he practices to this day. Over the years I had heard many times that Mrs. Astor had made Marciano promise that he would never leave her until she died—and that's a promise that Marciano had made and intended to keep. He would vacation in Portugal during the summer, but when Mrs. Astor still could travel to Maine, Marciano would always come back the last two weeks of her stay to drive her around, take walks, have lunch together. He just took very good care of her.

But in August 2005, Mr. Marshall called me from Maine and told me that he was letting Marciano go. He said that Mrs. Astor didn't need a chauffeur anymore, and if she had to be driven somewhere, Luis—Mr. Marshall's chauffeur—could drive her. I was overwhelmed. I just couldn't believe Marciano was being fired. I felt this was a giant step in eliminating an important person in her life, and totally unnecessary.

Now, Mr. Marshall earlier had asked me whether I knew if Marciano was living in the small East 72nd Street apartment that came with the job. I had no idea. Mrs. Astor owned the apartment, and it was always given to her chauffeur to live in. Mr. Marshall said he thought Marciano had a girlfriend, and maybe he was living with her. I said I had no way of knowing. (I later found out that Mr. Marshall wanted to give the apartment to Charlene's son Robert.)

So when Mr. Marshall fired Marciano, the apartment was a problem. The previous chauffeur had had an agreement in letter form that if he was let go, Mrs. Astor would allow him three months to vacate the apartment, and Marciano thought that he would get the same consideration. Mr. Marshall wanted him out in one month, but I believe Marciano eventually got a month and a half to pack up and go. Just before his last day, Marciano told me he met with Mrs. Astor and explained that he had to leave. It took her a while to understand what he was saying, but when she did, her eyes just overflowed with tears. The two of them sat in her apartment and cried together. He should never have been let go. He was Mrs. Astor's link to the outside world—a drive through town, a drive to Central Park. Those things disappeared with Marciano.

What did Mr. Marshall get out of all this? Well, he saved Marciano's salary—and immediately hired a captain for his new million-dollar yacht, which he named the *General Russell*, after his grandfather. The captain's salary of $70,000 per year, of course, was to be paid by Mrs. Astor, though she couldn't have known it. And Mr. Marshall gained an apartment on 72nd Street for Charlene's son Robert to live in. (Ironically, the story I got after my departure was that when Robert had a good look at the apartment, he decided it was too small for him.)

Well, it didn't take an Einstein to see the handwriting on the wall for me. From the beginning of the year I had felt that Mr. Marshall was trying to make things so unpleasant for me that I would quit and he wouldn't have the bother of firing me. When Charlene spoke to me...she was barely civil, but mostly she just didn't speak to me at all. They baited all of us with complaints or petty chores that we could never perform to their satisfaction.

In May 2005, Mr. Marshall came in and told Lourdes and me, "I'm sorry I ever gave you those Friday afternoons off in the summer." Some years before, Charlene had suggested that he close the office at 1 p.m. on summer Fridays, and we were thrilled with this benefit. Charlene was a normal working person then, still executive director of the Garden Club of America, and she got Mr. Marshall to give us the half-day off. In fact, Lourdes and I would alternate each week taking a full day off on Fridays and counting it as a half-day of vacation. This went on for many years. All of New York seems to close down on summer Fridays anyway; our phones never rang, and it made no sense for both of us to be in the office. We could never reach anyone on Friday afternoons either. But now Mr. Marshall was telling us he was sorry he had been kind to us! Why would he say such a thing? He never gave us an explanation. He just regretted being so considerate. How odd. At the beginning of the next summer 2006, almost a year after I had been fired, he told Lourdes and the person who replaced me that if they took a Friday off, they would be charged with a full day's vacation. He said that I "had taken advantage" of the practice, and that's why he was changing it. He couldn't say Lourdes was at fault—she was still there in front of him. But I was gone, so naturally he blamed me for it. And I thought to myself, *There's something wrong with him.* He could have come out years earlier and said he didn't want Lourdes or me to take half-day Fridays off, but he never did. This was part of the Marshalls' total attitude change that I had felt—first by Charlene, but then it had rubbed off on Mr. Marshall. I might add that in the entire twelve years of my employment, I don't believe I took more than twelve days off for personal reasons such as illness, funerals, or being caught out of town during a snowstorm! I was a very dependable employee.

A few weeks after this announcement in 2005, the Marshalls went off to Maine for the summer. Every summer for years I had volunteered to pick up their personal mail at their apartment and FedEx it to them in Maine. It wasn't a problem for me. I lived fairly near their apartment, so I could pick it up on the way to work or grab a cab during the day and run up to their place a couple of times a week. That summer of 2005, however, I couldn't seem to manage the chore correctly. Mr. Marshall would call and, in an annoyed tone, complain that I hadn't sent *all* the mail. Now the elevator in their apartment building was being repaired, so the doorman kept the Marshalls' mail in a box in the lobby. That's where I collected the mail. One day Mr. Marshall called to complain that I hadn't sent up the three Netflix movies. What Netflix? They weren't in the box. Mr. Marshall insisted I go back the next day and get them. The next day I picked up the mail, but…no Netflix. Now, I knew Charlene's son, Robert, was staying in their apartment that summer, and the building porter had his work number. I asked him to call Robert to inquire for me. Sure enough, Robert told him that the Netflix were in the apartment, and I shouldn't worry— he would send them up to Maine. I returned to the office and called the Marshalls in Maine and left a phone message for Mr. Marshall explaining the situation, saying that Robert would send them up to Maine himself. Mr. Marshall called back and said no, no, no—I was to go back the next day (this is three trips, three days in a row) and get the Netflix. So I went back. The Netflix envelopes were open; Robert obviously had been watching the movies.

Was this my fault for not sending those movies up to the Marshalls earlier? Was his insistence on getting them *right away* a joke? Nope. No joke. And it was *my* fault for not sending up the Netflix that were in Robert's possession. It's those little annoyances that can make you furious. I was furious.

Anyway, given this and all the staff firings, I was not entirely unprepared when Mr. Marshall returned from Maine on September 6 and called me into his office the next day. He closed the door. He fired me. I had known it was coming. I had seen what had happened to so many others loyal to Mrs. Astor. Still, it was a shock. I was surprised at how much of a shock it actually was—like being hit with a baseball bat. He told me that he had realized over the summer that he had so much work of his own to be done that he needed someone who could take shorthand and who was more computer savvy! At that point I had been there 12 years, and he never had mentioned those requirements before. I always took "fast longhand" when he needed to send correspondence, and I could have taken a course if he needed more computer work. I used the computer mainly for correspondence and check writing. If he had wanted me to learn other functions, I was game. But I knew he really just needed some excuse to get rid of me. He offered me $15,000 as a severance. Even in my state of shock, I still knew that sounded extremely meager for someone with no retirement fund. I negotiated with him and wound up with a year's salary, including medical insurance. Believe me, the atmosphere in that office during the past year was so depressing that I was not unhappy to be leaving...except that I knew that Lourdes, my dear friend, would be upset.

And, I actually felt betrayed. Even though I disapproved of many things I had witnessed in Mr. Marshall's actions, I was still a dedicated employee who guarded his privacy and put 100% effort into my responsibilities. I thought there was a trust between us. But he dismissed me without a thought of my future. I guess I had been naïve.

Mr. Marshall told Lourdes that he was letting me go and asked her advice on my severance. She backed me up, so that's probably why he agreed to my request. And I was concerned about Mrs. Astor having one fewer of her long-term employees eyeballing the situation. I believe that I was fired mostly because Mrs. Marshall wanted me *out* and someone loyal to the Marshalls *in*. As it turned out, the Marshalls had hired my replacement in early July—so that summer, when Mr. Marshall was sending me back and forth to his apartment to collect his mail, he already knew he was firing me. Then I was even more certain that he had been hoping I would resign and save him the trouble—not to mention my severance.

That was the end of my employment by Mrs. Astor, but, as I soon found out, it was just the beginning of a new chapter in the story. I was still "decompressing" from the experience when I got a call from a woman named Frances Kiernan, a writer who was working on a biography of Mrs. Astor. I vaguely remembered meeting her in the office years before, when she had come in to interview Mrs. Astor or Mr. Marshall. Linda Gillies had given her my name. Ms. Kiernan, who had been fiction editor of The *New Yorker* magazine for many years and had written a biography of Mary McCarthy, said she would like to interview me about my employment with Mrs. Astor and Mr. Marshall.

Now, over the last two and a half years that I had been with Mrs. Astor's office, I had kept extensive notes about everything I had seen that made me suspicious. I thought I would maybe write a book about it myself someday, and I wanted a record of what had happened. So when Frances Kiernan called, I said I would be happy to talk to her, and I went to her home—she has a lovely apartment on Park Avenue in the 90s—and we got acquainted. She's a striking woman in her sixties with dramatic white hair, but she has very youthful skin, so she looks much younger than her years. I enjoyed the presence of her magnificent cats as we chatted and had tea. Frances had interviewed Mrs. Astor several times but had noticed quite a change between the first interview and the last, when Mrs. Astor couldn't seem to remember things. She also had interviewed many of Mrs. Astor's friends, and some of them had indicated that things weren't quite right. She told me that she originally had intended to write a book about Mrs. Astor's life as a philanthropist and her experiences as head of the Vincent Astor Foundation. As the months went by and more details of Mrs. Astor's condition surfaced, Frances began to revise her book. She and I would talk many more times.

In December 2005, three months after I had been let go, I e-mailed Mr. Marshall and asked for permission to visit Mrs. Astor to take her a little Christmas gift, and he consented. She always loved Christmas, and decorated her apartment and Holly Hill beautifully. So on December 16 I went up to 778 Park with a pretty ornament for her tree. On the way I remembered something that Mrs. Astor had said at one of the last Christmas parties she threw for the staff before the foundation was closed. We all were sitting around, and the conversation turned to our plans for the holiday. Mrs. Astor said that Mr. Marshall would be spending Christmas "with his family"—meaning Charlene and her three children—but she herself had nothing to do on the holiday. "My family is in heaven," Mrs. Astor said, and I thought it was just so sad. She meant her mother and father and her husbands, I guess, but it was a bit uncomfortable to hear her say that. I mean, Mr. Marshall was sitting right there—he and Charlene had been married for six or seven years at that point—and didn't she consider them part of her family? Hadn't they invited her? Hadn't she invited them? It was an unsettling moment for me, so I can just imagine how Mr. Marshall felt.

All that was going through my mind when I reached Mrs. Astor's apartment. Mily let me in, and I was struck by how quiet the place seemed. There were no Christmas decorations of any kind, but in an adjoining room there was a small Christmas tree on a table that had been brought in by Mrs. Astor's faithful friend and "adopted daughter" Annette de la Renta. Then I was shown in to see Mrs. Astor. She was sitting in a chair, beautifully dressed, made up, and wearing her jewels, but I thought she looked terribly frail. I told her who I was, but I didn't tell her I had been let go. I said that I was Alice, from her business office, and that I paid her bills, etc... and I assured her that she had plenty of money, not to fret, because she always worried about that and I didn't want her to be concerned. I talked about how she used to come to the office and I reminded her of stories we had told together, people we worked with...you know, just chit-chat. On some visits I would do a little dance for her because I knew she loved to dance, and that would just *perk* her right up. I can't remember whether I danced this time. I stayed maybe 30 or 40 minutes, and at the end I thought she knew who I was. She asked me please to come back and visit her again. But I wasn't on the list—the very short list—of people Mr. Marshall would want to visit. I went away with a heavy heart, knowing that Mrs. Astor wasn't getting the stimulation she needed to stay alert.

Part of me thought that, well, Mr. Marshall just didn't want people to see his mother in her diminished condition. But it also seemed to me that her close friends would be happy to visit and just talk to her, maybe read to her for a while. I know I would have been glad to do that. She was isolated and alone, and she seemed to respond only to Mily. It appeared to me that Mily was her security—a constant she recognized. Her flowers and all the amenities she was used to were gone—perhaps Mr. Marshall assumed she wasn't able to appreciate them anymore. Or maybe he was just penny-pinching as usual. I recall that over the last couple of years that I was employed I got at least two calls from other employees who said Mr. Marshall said to them, "Well, there's not much money left." That was ridiculous. There was plenty. How could he say such a thing?

Then, just a few weeks later, shortly after New Year's 2006, I got that fateful phone call from Philip Marshall that

I described at the beginning of this book. What a relief! Finally I could tell my entire story to someone who was concerned and who maybe could make a difference. Over the next few months I spoke to Philip often. I told him, "Your grandmother's legacy has been totally changed," and that's what bothered him. That's what bothered *me*. Mrs. Astor had spelled out what she wanted in her will, and her wishes were being completely altered.

I don't think either Philip or his brother, Alec, ever had been particularly close to their grandmother, but, in the last five or six years that I was there, things changed. Philip visited her a lot more, and she liked his family. I remember Mrs. Astor telling me that Philip's children were very well-mannered, and she liked them. They visited her at Holly Hill, and whenever Philip was in New York on business or whatever, he would stop by to see his grandmother.

Now let me make this clear: In my opinion, Philip's actions were never motivated by money. Number one, he's not that kind of person; he doesn't lead a big, ostentatious life. He's a college professor. He told me that some time ago he went to his father and said, "Look, Nan and I"—Nan is his wife— "Nan and I are doing our wills, and I'm trying to get everything set. We've already spoken to Nan's family, and they have told us what to expect to inherit from them. So I have to ask you what I can expect from Grandmother so I can figure it all out." Mr. Marshall told him, "Your grandmother was leaving you and your brother $10,000 each." *Wait a minute! That's crazy*, is what I thought when I heard this. *$10,000?* But Philip told me that Charlene then stepped into the conversation and told him, "Don't worry. Your father has changed that, and now you and Alec will each receive $1 million when she dies."

Look at it this way: If Philip were really after the money when he filed the initial petition with the court, he should have let the latest will go through unchallenged—he would have gotten $1 million instead of $10,000. (Philip later found out that in the last several wills it had always been $1 million!) But the more he thought about it, the more Charlene's information disturbed him. He told me, "I started thinking: How did he do that? How did he change the will? If I'm getting a million and Alec is getting a million, does this mean that my father and Charlene are getting all the rest?" I was worried that Mrs. Astor's intentions had been changed. I said that most of what Mrs. Astor has is probably going to go to your father, then to Charlene, and then to Charlene's three children. "If anything," I added, "the money should go to you and your children and to Alec and his daughter." But Philip said to me, "I don't want the money. But I *really* don't think Charlene should inherit *all* the money."

So while I was talking to Philip and telling him everything suspicious I had seen, he also was speaking to other employees and friends of Mrs. Astor's. He consulted lawyers. But months went by, and it looked as if nothing was going to happen. No one wanted the story to go public, for one thing, and, given her age, how much time did Mrs. Astor have left? Philip was being told he should wait until his grandmother died and then challenge the will.

But Philip was hearing more and more detailed information about Mrs. Astor's diminished lifestyle and the lavish spending of the Marshalls. He decided he had to go forward while his grandmother was still alive. He wanted to make sure that Mrs. Astor was being well cared for—cared for in a manner befitting her life, and he wanted her legacy to be what she intended. So Philip hired Ira Salzman, a New York attorney who specializes in elder law, and enlisted David Rockefeller and Annette de la Renta, Mrs. Astor's two dearest friends, to help him. One factor may have encouraged the two to help Philip: Mr. Marshall had once again shut down Holly Hill, marooning Mrs. Astor in New York, just as he had the summer before, when only Mr. Rockefeller's and Annette's intervention had changed his mind. The two of them must have been outraged. And that's how it came about that on July 20, 2006, the legal papers were filed, accusing Mr. Marshall of neglecting his mother and misappropriating her funds for his own benefit.

Then all hell broke loose! And it happened in a particularly messy way. The court ordered Mr. Marshall removed as his mother's guardian and gave temporary custody to Mrs. de la Renta. Mr. Marshall also was stripped of his role as Mrs. Astor's financial manager, and her fortune was placed under the guardianship of the JPMorgan Chase bank.

Mr. Marshall and Charlene were up at Cove End, in Maine for the summer. They didn't even know the petition had been filed! The plan was for Philip to inform his father of these secret actions a few days later, on July 25. But suddenly Mrs. Astor fell ill with pneumonia and had to be rushed to the hospital in the wee hours of Monday, July 24. Mr. Marshall had to be notified. So Philip called his father in Maine on Monday and said Mrs. Astor was seriously ill in the hospital...and, by the way, I've filed a petition against you for neglecting my grandmother, and you're no longer her guardian or financial manager.

Can you only imagine? That must have been some diffi-cult phone call to make. Mr. Marshall was livid and denied everything. Charlene quickly got on the phone and said to Philip, "What have you *done*? How could you do this to your father?" They were on the next plane back to New York, but things had begun to move quickly.

By court order, the locks were changed on the office door at 405 Park Avenue and at Mrs. Astor's apartment. Mr. Marshall was literally locked out. Mrs. de la Renta saw to it that the sheets were whisked off the furniture at Holly Hill, and Mrs. Astor's country estate was opened up again. Chris

Ely, her loyal butler, was rehired, as were her former cook and housekeeper. When Mrs. Astor was released from the hospital, an ambulance took her to her beautiful country home, with nurses in attendance, where she would live out her days in the house she loved so much.

Within a day or two of Philip filing the suit, the story was leaked to the press, probably by someone at the courthouse, and—*KABOOM!*—it was front-page news everywhere. It had all the elements of a juicy scandal about the rich and famous. Every day there was a new tidbit of information. Mr. Marshall accused his son Philip of betraying him and ruining everything. Others defended Philip and his motives, saying his grandmother was living in squalor and sleeping on "a pee-stained sofa." The media were relentless. I was getting calls from all the newspapers and TV stations in New York, and some reporters were hanging around my apartment building trying to get an interview. Thank goodness for doormen! None of the staff wanted to talk, and for the most part we didn't.

But on July 27, 2006 *The New York Times* ran an article that really got my goat. It was an interview with David Richenthal, the Marshalls' partner in Delphi, their theatrical production company. Richenthal told the *Times* that he had worked in Mrs. Astor's apartment for two years, and the apartment was lovely and well maintained. Mrs. Astor, he said, was well cared for. Everything there was hunky-dory.

He said that Mrs. Astor had Alzheimer's—which no one had spoken of publicly—but that she still had her social secretary. And he claimed that Mr. Marshall's only indulgence was a small motorboat.

Well, I saw red. What really ticked me off was Richenthal saying Mrs. Astor had Alzheimer's, which no one had ever said to the public. Ever. It wasn't for him to say, number one. Number two, if she had Alzheimer's, did she give him permission to have an office in her apartment, while she paid all the expenses? (The Marshalls, who obviously had been the source of Richenthal's Alzheimer's claim, backtracked on this--if she had Alzheimer's could she have signed the codicils to her will?) And why didn't Richenthal mention that the Marshalls had hired Erica Meyer as Mrs. Astor's "social secretary" when she actually worked mostly as an assistant for Delphi? Did he pay for her salary and expenses? Didn't they charge all that to Mrs. Astor? Finally, if the Marshalls' only indulgence was "a small boat," why did they need a captain—which Mrs. Astor also was paying for?

So I felt I needed to counter what Richenthal was saying, and when Serge Kovaleski, a reporter for the *Times*, called, I said I was very upset by what had been written. I agreed to be interviewed and I told him my story, which appeared in *The New York Times* on August 1, 2006. He turned out to be an excellent investigative reporter, and he was very respectful of what I told him, both on and off the record. Unfortunately, several other newspapers picked up my quotes and changed the words to make it sound more sensational. I talked to Serge several more times but not in full interviews-- only to give him guidance in his own investigations.

Meanwhile, in the summer of 2006 Philip's lawyers and JPMorgan Chase called me to their offices to help explain bills I had paid over the years. My stories seemed to fascinate everyone, and since I had kept notes about things that perturbed me, I had quite the tale to tell. Several people said to me, "This is such a made-for-TV movie!!" So I knew I had to put it all down on paper, and that's how this book began. I went through one bill after another, explaining what it was for and whether it was paid for Mrs. Astor's benefit or not. The Marshalls' co-op apartment bills in New York, for instance, were paid by Mrs. Astor. After the Marshalls took ownership of Cove End in Maine, the bills there were paid by Mrs. Astor. The salaries of the maid and cook the Marshalls brought to Cove End from Antigua, their airline tickets and their uniforms were paid for by Mrs. Astor. And I won't even go into the small stuff—the $100 here and $200 there for groceries, FedEx, messengers, whatever—Mrs. Astor's money paid for all of it.

So I was sent a subpoena to testify at the Supreme Court of the State of New York regarding Philip's petition. How strange it felt. I wasn't looking forward to seeing the Marshalls, but all of us who had been on the staff had stories to tell and had to have our day in court. However, a settlement was reached on October 13, 2006, so that was that.

In the 18-page settlement that was approved by Justice John E. H. Stackhouse, Mr. Marshall was not found guilty of elder abuse, but he agreed that the custody of his mother should go permanently to Annette de la Renta and JP Morgan Chase. So there was obviously a deal reached. We all assumed that nothing would happen further until Mrs. Astor died and her will was challenged.

Then one day in November 2006 I was walking down Lexington Avenue when my cell phone rang. It was a man named Don Kennedy, who explained that he was an investigator with the district attorney's office, and they would like to talk to me. I was like...*uwwww*...what's this about? He said I was to go downtown to 1 Hogan Place, the DA's office in New York County's Criminal Court Building, and speak to a woman named Elizabeth Loewy, who was the assistant DA handling Financial Elder Abuse. So I made an appointment and went to see them, and I remember there were two Assistant DAs, Liz Loewy and Peirce Moser; Don Kennedy; and one administrative assistant present. They worked in the typical back rooms of a municipal building. It looked like an old school building—makeshift, you know, some tables and what-have-you. Nothing fancy, for sure.

They started asking questions, and basically they just wanted to know about my years working for Mrs. Astor. I told them, "You just ask me the questions, and I'll tell you what I know." So I went on and on about my stories, and they were amazed. They wanted all my notes, and so I said I would give them copies, which I did. I copied them, and Don Kennedy picked them up at my apartment.

The DA's office called me back in April 2007, but it was basically to go over some things I had told them in November. They were investigating, and it takes a long time to go through everything. They obviously were interviewing everybody else involved. I certainly wasn't the only one. They interviewed *everybody*. I understood that they were going to give all this information to a Grand Jury, but I heard nothing until Serge Kovaleski of *The New York Times* called me in July. I was up at my house on Cape Cod, and Serge asked me if I had been called by the Grand Jury. I said nobody had called me. Then one of the other employees called me—I believe it was Chris Ely—and said he had been called to testify before the Grand Jury. I naively thought, "Well, maybe they don't need my testimony," but, sure enough, I also got a call shortly thereafter to go before the Grand Jury.

Now all the testimony before a Grand Jury is secret, so none of us who were called ever talked about what we were asked. Lourdes and I were there on the same day, but we never discussed what we talked about. In fact, Alec Marshall was also testifying that day, so we all met in the anteroom before taking our turns. Alec had tried to remain neutral throughout the ordeal, but he still had to testify. The assistant DA, Liz Loewy, was in charge, and she asked me questions. I answered them, and that was that. At the end, members of the Grand Jury--I think there were 20 or more there--were able to ask me questions through the assistant DA. They had a lot of questions, and I was glad to see they were paying attention. They weren't sleeping, by any means. When, in November 2007, they came out with the indictments against Mr. Marshall, I was overwhelmed by how tough they were. But I'll get to that in the next chapter.

Meanwhile, during all those months, Mrs. Astor was just fading away. I was able to visit her twice during her last months, and I was glad to see that she was being so well taken care of in the house she loved so much. The last time I saw her was on April 28, 2007. I visited her with my husband Joe. It was kind of ghostly to walk through the halls of Holly Hill, with all the photographs of Mrs. Astor next to so many well-known people. Joe said it was like a tour of the history of the twentieth century, and it was. She had seen it all.

I talked to her as I always had, just chitchat, but I don't think she knew who I was. She was obviously failing. I also sang to her the little song she had sung to me about the bridge in Avignon years before. I thought it might spark a memory. The two nurses who were in attendance told me that sometimes, late in the day, she might comment about something that had happened earlier in the day, so no one knew for sure what she was grasping. I left there knowing I would probably not see her again.

She died on August 13, 2007 at the age of 105. She had asked that her tombstone read: I HAD A WONDERFUL LIFE

CHAPTER NINE

DEATH AND BEYOND

───◦∞◦───

I got an e-mail from Philip about an hour after Mrs. Astor had died, telling me of her passing. Obviously, I was prepared for her death, but it still seemed unreal. She had gone on for so long and had weathered so many crises, it seemed as if she would live forever. I just started every day thinking she would always be there. Now, the fight over her legacy was about to enter a new phase.

The tributes to this extraordinary woman went on for days and weeks on TV, in newspapers, and in magazines. The *New York Times*, in its front-page obituary, which continued for a full page inside, called her the "Wry Aristocrat of the People," which was a very accurate summation. It mentioned her practice of dressing every day in a designer dress, hat, gloves, makeup, and jewelry—whether she were going to a board meeting at the Metropolitan Museum of Art or to a local charity in Harlem to dine off paper plates—something I had seen over the 12 years I had worked for her. Charlie Rose, a close friend of Mrs. Astor's, devoted one of his shows to her, including an interview he had done with her when she was in her nineties. After watching the show, a male friend of mine told me he now could see how she captivated men—she was flirtatious, down-to-earth, and utterly charming. He said you could see that she loved men, and you could see why men loved her in turn.

I read in the newspapers that Mr. Marshall was in charge of his mother's funeral arrangements, and I knew that there would be a guest list at St. Thomas Episcopal Church on Fifth Avenue at 53rd Street. The papers reported there were 415 people on the list. I really wanted to go, but I also knew that I wouldn't be on the list. I didn't want to bother Philip about it because I knew the situation would be uncomfortable and tense for him. So I just didn't go, and now I kick myself for it, because I heard only about half of the church's 1,800 seats were filled-- which would *not* have pleased Mrs. Astor--and I later found out I could have gone in with one of the employees who was invited. I think the service actually was opened to the public, but many people obviously thought the way I did—that you had to be on the guest list. The Marine Corps provided an honor guard as her casket was taken out of the church. She was buried the next day at Sleepy Hollow Cemetery with only the Marshalls and a minister present.

Six weeks later, the Metropolitan Museum of Art dedicated a weekend (September 28-30) to a tribute to Mrs. Astor, and I was delighted to be invited to the opening lecture on Friday night and a reception afterwards given by Mrs. de la Renta. My husband was out of town, so I asked my sister, Susan Cooper, to go with me, and we had a grand time. As we were about to enter for the lecture, I noticed Mr. Marshall and Charlene going into the auditorium. I didn't want to come face to face with them, so Susan and I sat on the opposite side of the room. The Marshalls were in the front row, just below the podium on the right side of the hall. Philippe de Montebello, the longtime head of the Metropolitan Museum, spoke first, and he introduced Lord William Astor, representing the English branch of the Astor family. Lord Astor told some funny stories about Mrs. Astor, and, at the end of his remarks, pointedly thanked David Rockefeller and Annette de la Renta for taking such good care of her. The featured speaker was Maxwell K. Hearn, the Douglas Dillon Curator of Chinese Painting and Calligraphy in the Met's Department of Asian Art. He showed slides and praised Mrs. Astor for her many gifts, including the Chinese garden and surrounding rooms, now known as the Astor Court, which is one of the more sensational exhibits in the vast Metropolitan. At the end, he also thanked Mrs. de la Renta for her care of Mrs. Astor. It was obvious where they stood in the de la Renta/Marshall face-off!

After the lecture, those of us invited to the reception convened upstairs in a private room for drinks and hors d'oeuvres, and

I was so happy to finally meet some of the people with whom I had spoken on the phone over the years but never had a chance to meet in the flesh. Mrs. Astor's great-granddaughter Hilary Marshall, who is Alec's daughter, turned out to be a charming young woman of 17. I had been sending her birthday and Christmas cards and checks from Mrs. Astor since she was a young child, and now she was getting ready to go off to college!

I met Dwight Johnson and his assistant, Denise, lovely people from the Black Alumni of Pratt Institute, which Mrs. Astor had always supported. I met Mrs. Astor's nurse, Minnette Christie, who had been so amazed at Mrs. Astor's vigor and drive when she cared for her in 1998 after she broke her hip for the first time. She hadn't been able to believe the energy and will of a 96-year-old woman!

I met Annette de la Renta for the first time. We certainly knew of each other, but had never met in person. I was surprised at how petite she is. And, I got to speak with Lord Astor and meet his wife and son who accompanied him.

I also met Mrs. Astor's court-appointed lawyer, Susan Robbins, who had represented her in the controversy over her guardianship and who referred the case to the criminal court after suspecting that the signature on the third codicil was forged. And there was a very pregnant Naomi Packard Dunn-Koot, who was Mrs. Astor's former social secretary, as well as photographer Bill Cunningham of the *New York Times*, who had been photographing Mrs. Astor for eons! The evening left me feeling quite happy that we all were celebrating Mrs. Astor and her enormous legacies to the Metropolitan Museum of Art. It was an uplifting experience.

Now at that time the Metropolitan and many other New York institutions were waiting to see what the courts would decide about Mrs. Astor's 2002 will and the codicils that had been added to it. They had been filed in the Surrogate's Court in Westchester County right after her death. Mr. Marshall wanted the 2002 will and codicils to be enforced, while Philip and Mrs. Astor's guardians wanted the 1997 will enforced since that was the last one she signed before there was any question of her competency. It was reported that Mrs. Astor would leave a fortune of some $130 million, in addition to the Vincent Astor Trust of some $60 million, which she planned to leave to her favorite charities. Mrs. Astor intended to leave millions to the Metropolitan Musuem, the New York Public Library, New York University, etc...and she had told them what to expect. But now, if the 2002 will and codicils added in 2003 and 2004 were upheld, all those institutions stood to receive millions less than they had expected. Her 2001 will, for example, had left the Childe Hassam painting, *Flags*, to the Met, but Mr. Marshall already had sold it—and a new will was written in 2002. Anyway, the state's Attorney General's office had ordered a halt to talks to resolve the dispute over the wills because of the criminal allegations against Mr. Marshall. Everyone was waiting for the next shoe to drop, and they didn't have long to wait.

I was driving home from Cape Cod after Thanksgiving weekend, 2007, when I got a call from Chris Ely, who told me he had just seen online that Mr. Marshall and the lawyer, Francis X. Morrissey Jr., had been indicted on criminal charges. One of the charges in the 18-count indictment accused both men of exploiting Mrs. Astor in her last years so that they could gain financially. One count charged both men of conspiring to amend Mrs. Astor's will to leave much of her estate to Mr. Marshall rather than to charity. One accused Morrissey of forging Mrs. Astor's signature on the third codicil to her 2002 will. I wasn't surprised by the indictments, but I was surprised that I suddenly felt bad for Mr. Marshall. I mean, here was an 83-year-old man facing criminal charges and possibly prison, and I'm sure he still felt that he hadn't done anything wrong. Phone calls began flying from every direction—other former employees, the media, family, friends—I could barely keep up. All I could say to people was that it just felt unreal that it had finally come to this. I'm sure Philip Marshall must have felt bad, too. He certainly didn't want his father to go to jail. He just wanted Mrs. Astor and her legacy to be treated fairly.

A couple of weeks later, on December 10, 2007, I went to Barnes & Noble to hear Frances Kiernan give a talk on her book, *The Last Mrs. Astor*, which had been published in May 2007. I was surprised—and Fran was even more surprised—to see Charlene Marshall in the audience. During the question-and-answer session after Fran's talk, Charlene got up and asked questions—which were more like statements. It was outrageous! I had to bite my tongue not to jump up and challenge what she said about the Vincent Astor Foundation.

Since I had taken over administering the foundation after it closed its doors to the public in 1997, I was very well versed in what had happened since that time. Charlene, however, asked Frances Kiernan why she hadn't mentioned in the book that Mr. Marshall had kept $3 million in foundation money for Mrs. Astor to continue to give away for another year after the foundation officially closed. Charlene said Mr. Marshall had invested the money so well that it doubled in value and allowed Mrs. Astor to give away money for another five years. Fran replied that Mr. Marshall had asked her not to include that in the book.

Well, first of all, he kept $2 million, not $3 million, and it did not double in value. I don't have the exact figures, but since I wrote all the checks and kept a log, I would have noticed if there had been that much more to give away. And why didn't Charlene mention that many of the grants made during that time were designed to benefit the Marshalls? I was dying to point out, for instance, that one bequest of $5,000 was made to the Juilliard School of Music; Charlene was on the school's advisory council, which required her to make a $5,000 donation—but it was made not by her but by the Vincent Astor Foundation. How about the $25,000 grant to St. James' Church, at Madison Avenue and 71st Street, toward a new organ? Charlene was a member of the church, not Mrs. Astor. Then there was the $15,000 given to the Metropolitan Opera, which conveniently satisfied Mr. Marshall's obligation as an opera Patron. The Marshalls co-chaired an event at the American Museum of Natural History, which required them to purchase a $50,000 table. Did they pay for it? No, the foundation did. All these organizations deserved the money, but it was the Marshalls whose social status benefited.

I could go on and on, but you get the point. I didn't want to add to Fran Kiernan's stress at the event by challenging Charlene, so I kept my mouth shut. The next day there was an article in the New York *Post* about the encounter. I knew that if I had opened my mouth, that article would have been explosive!

After Mrs. Astor died, and her wills and codicils were filed, I started going back over all the papers I had received from Philip. During the months we had corresponded, I would send him or tell him information that I thought he should know; he, in turn, would send me anything that he thought confirmed some of my suspicions—including the wills and codicils. There was so much material that I hadn't gone through it all, and a lot of it I had read just once, very quick-ly. Now I sat down to read it all at leisure. I noticed that Philip had sent me a copy of the 2001 will and of the 2002 will, and I read them for the first time. Their contents were eye opening!

To my surprise, I was mentioned in the 2001 will—Mrs. Astor had left me $10,000. In fact, several employees were left amounts of $10,000, or $25,000, or even $50,000. Even more surprising was when more recently I gained access to the 1997 will and found out I was in that one too for $10,000.

But in the 2002 will, only two employees were named to receive specific amounts—Steve Hamor and Chris Ely were being left $50,000 each. The 2002 will also includes a state-ment by Mrs. Astor, saying, "I have made arrangements for my other long-time employees whose employment will end with my death." *Hmmmm.* I wondered what those arrange-ments were. Why had they been changed? In the earlier will, Mrs. Astor also had specified that certain pieces of her jewelry were to go to special people—a pin and earrings to Linda Gillies, the emeralds to Annette de la Renta, a pin and earrings to Charlene—but those instructions do not appear in the 2002 will. The later will was much kinder to Charlene than the original—for instance, she was finally to get the 367-diamond Van Cleef & Arpels "Snowflake" necklace I de-scribed earlier, which she had always coveted.

I often go over in my mind what happened in Mrs. Astor's world from 2002 to 2005, the last 2 ½ years I worked at 405 Park Avenue. It seems surreal that all the details were in the newspapers. During those years all the strange doings were only whispered about among Mrs. Astor's employees, and none of us knew what to do about them. Now the public knows so much.

I've listened to the remarks of those who read about the scandal in the newspapers, and many of them just didn't understand why Mr. Marshall was in such trouble. He was her only son, they said--why shouldn't he inherit everything? Well, the short answer is: Because that's not what Mrs. Astor intended. It was *her* right to decide, not Mr. Marshall's right, or Francis X. Morrissey's right. None of this ever should have happened; it wasn't necessary. Mrs. Astor intended to leave plenty of money for her son and his wife to live on very comfortably for the rest of their lives. But I suspected they wanted more. They wanted it all. It had to be pure greed. And perhaps some measure of revenge.

Even in the most loving parent/child relationships, there always is some undercurrent of resentment or anger. That's just a fact of life. I don't know what Mrs. Astor's relationship to her son was like before I arrived, but it certainly seemed "odd" to me after I had a chance to observe it for a while. As much as I revered Mrs. Astor, I certainly saw many instances of her disregard for her son's feelings. She didn't seem to realize how hurtful she could be to him. It was uncomfortable, for instance, to hear her say, as I previously mentioned, she couldn't spend Christmas with her family because they all were in heaven—while Mr. Marshall was sitting there listening to her. He was family, wasn't he? He must have resented that. He must have resented his mother writing that he was a "wretched" student in her autobiography, *Footprints*. Couldn't she have cushioned that and many other comments about him?

So maybe Mr. Marshall's attempts to grab his mother's money reflected some form of payback. Payback for the time and attention she admitted she didn't give him as a child. Payback for his biological father's never caring about him. Payback for Vincent Astor's dislike of him, for his stepfather's attempts to ruin his relationship with his mother, and for his mother's acquiescence in Vincent's disdain. Payback for Mrs. Astor's refusal to accept with open arms his choice of Charlene as his third wife and for her ongoing coolness to her. And payback for Mrs. Astor not showing the exalted people in her world just how much she loved her son and how proud she was of him. Well, I'm not qualified--maybe no one is--to analyze the psychology of their relationship, but Mr. Marshall must have believed he had ample cause to resent the way his mother sometimes treated him. He *must* have felt that the least his mother could do would be to leave him her entire fortune.

Meanwhile, there was no end to media coverage of the scandal. One of the most damning reports was a long article by Serge Kovaleski and Colin Moynihan in the *New York Times* on January 4, 2008 about the strange career of Francis X. Morrissey Jr., the attorney indicted along with Mr. Marshall. According to the *Times* article, Morrissey had a curious knack for befriending wealthy elderly people, who then would change their wills to leave much of their estates to him. Working often with two other New York lawyers, Warren J. Forsythe and Peter J. Kelley, Morrissey had involved himself "in several dozen estates over three decades," *The Times* said. In 1997, for instance, Mr. Forsythe had drafted a new will for an elderly widow. When she died in 2000 at 91, Morrissey inherited much of her $15 million estate, including her six-room apartment on Park Avenue. Her relatives and a probate official challenged the will, *The Times* continued, but Morrissey still walked away with "a significant portion" of her assets.

The article went on to document many other similar cases involving Morrissey, who once had been suspended from practicing law in New York State by the Appellate Division of the State Supreme Court for misappropriating almost a million dollars from an escrow fund. The parallels to Mrs. Astor's situation were pointed, and the article mentioned that Morrissey was "the primary contact and treasurer" of a foundation set up by Charlene in 2002—the Shepherd Community Foundation. Charlene was president of the foundation, which had been financed by $100,000 from Mrs. Astor. Morrissey's lawyer denied he had done anything improper in reference to any of the estates.

On January 12, 2008, an article appeared in the *Wall Street Journal* about the problem Mrs. Astor's employees were facing in trying to get fair severance pay. I was happy to have spoken with the writer, Ianthe Jeanne Dugan, for the article. After JPMorgan Chase was appointed by the court as guardian for Mrs. Astor, the bank presented a severance plan to employees that gave them $1000 for each year of service, and the court approved it, but I don't believe the court was aware of prior severance packages such as mine. As I mentioned earlier, Mr. Marshall offered me $15,000, which I thought was an insult. I then negotiated a month's salary plus benefits for each year I had worked for him. Since I worked for twelve years, I got a year of salary as severance. I based my request on what the employees at the foundation had received when the foundation was closed, and on the severance given to a former social secretary.

I thought that there were several long-term employees who should have been treated the same way I was. Mrs. Astor's housekeeper, Mily de Gernier, was with her for more than 40 years, and Mrs. Astor used to tell her that she would take care of her for the rest of her life. Both Mr. Christensen and Mr. Marshall knew this, but it was never written down anywhere. For years, Mily would ask me about what she should do regarding this unwritten promise, and I always advised her to speak to Mr. Christensen—but then he was fired too.

But Mily, who's now more than 80 years old, shouldn't be worrying about how she's going to make ends meet. And my office colleague, Lourdes Hilario, worked for Mrs. Astor and Mr. Marshall for 22 years--she certainly should have received the same package I got.

And the three gardeners in Maine—Steve Hamor and his sons Scott and Steve Jr.—were particularly vulnerable. Steve Sr. worked at Cove End for more than 40 years and his sons for about 20 years. They probably didn't realize that once Cove End passed into Mr. Marshall's hands and then into Charlene's, they weren't working for Mrs. Astor anymore— their paychecks still came from her, even though they were working for the Marshalls. When JPMorgan Chase took over as temporary guardian of Mrs. Astor's assets, the bank immediately took the Hamors and all other people working for the Marshalls off of Mrs. Astor's payroll. Then Mr. Marshall fired the Hamors with no severance at all. Scott called me for advice, and all I could say was that he should call JPMorgan Chase and explain the situation.

The Hamors were unwitting pawns in all this, and their situation is heartbreaking. Scott told me that Mr. Marshall had talked to him and his dad at one point because he wanted to keep them on at Cove End, but let Steve Jr. go. They pleaded with him not to do that—Steve Jr. needed the money—and Mr. Marshall agreed, but eventually they all were dismissed.

Scott also told me that years ago Mrs. Astor had promised his father that he would stay on working at Cove End for five years after her death. Even after that, she said, he could continue to use the greenhouse and cutting garden so he could make a living. Of course, none of this was written down, but I have no doubt it's true. These are not people who make up such stories. But now all those promises seem to have gone up in smoke.

Then there's Alicia Johnson, who had been Mrs. Astor's housekeeper at Cove End for 12 years before the Marshalls fired her in 2004. In her 2001 will, Mrs. Astor had left Alicia $25,000, but when Mr. Marshall fired her, all she got was $10,000. I feel that Alicia deserves at least what Mrs. Astor, who liked her and valued her, originally intended to give her. Then there are the people who weren't fired and continued to work for Mrs. Astor until her death, like those caring for her at Holly Hill. I do feel that Mrs. Astor appreciated everyone who worked for her, and she would be the first person to want her faithful employees to receive a just settlement. In her autobiography, *Footprints*, Mrs. Astor talked about the sale of the St. Regis hotel after Vincent died and how she "insisted on giving large severance pay" to the people who were "loyal and devoted to Vincent."

If dear Mrs. Astor were aware of what's been going on since her death, I'm sure she'd be doing the proverbial rollover in her grave! On the other hand, she might get one of those twinkle-eyed expressions on her face which I saw so often. I recall seeing her one day after she had seen the musical *Chicago* on Broadway. I asked her whether she had liked it, and she smiled and said, "Oh, it was very *naughty!*" There certainly has been a lot of naughtiness here, and naughty could be nice to Mrs. Astor. But she also believed in justice.

And justice must be done.

CHAPTER TEN

TRIAL BEGINS

———∞∞∞———

How strange. Jury selection finally started on March 30, 2009, Mrs. Astor's birthday. It had been scheduled originally for January, then February and then March 23rd. But it didn't get off the ground until the 30th. I spoke to Philip on that day after a long period of silence. Was Mrs. Astor having a last word from the grave? I think so. I had received a subpoena from Mr. Marshall's lawyers in December 2008 wanting all my notes, thoughts, whatever on Mrs. Astor. I had given all my notes to the DA's office and my understanding was that at some point they had to share them with Mr. Marshall's Lawyers. Fine. But I wasn't in the mood to copy everything again for anyone.

So I hired a lawyer, Eric Seiff, recommended by my brother-in-law Bernard Cooper, to deal with it, and he got the subpoena withdrawn. My hero, Eric. Instead, Mr. Marshall's lawyers wanted me to answer some questions through my lawyer, which I did. The questions didn't seem very significant to me and didn't cover topics I would have wanted to know from me if I were Mr. Marshall's lawyers.

In mid-December 2008, I was called into the DA's office at Hogan Place to meet with Joel Seidemann, who had recently been brought in as one of three prosecutors on the case. It was a long meeting, and we went over my story again. Joel was becoming familiar with the case, but wanted to hear the tale directly from me. Then I met Joel again, on March 11, and by then he had a good grasp of the case and had many questions for me. He told me I would come in one more time before I had to testify.

Of course, all along I had hoped Mr. Marshall would take a plea bargain and none of us would have to testify. But that was not in the cards. Mr. Marshall wanted to clear his name. I couldn't imagine what he was thinking except that he still didn't believe he had done anything wrong. Part of me continued to feel bad for him, but when I would review my notes I would become agitated and realize how bad the behavior had been on his part and what trauma he had put Lourdes and me through for a very long time.

As I said, Mr. Marshall used to justify to me everything he did, moneywise, for many years. But when the big change came in June 2003--the hip disaster--I think he justified only to himself what he was doing and that must have satisfied him. Lourdes and I would sometimes think perhaps he was having senility problems himself. And in our chats, we speculated that Mrs. Marshall was pulling the strings. Now, many former employees and people associated with Mrs. Astor were going to get up in court and answer questions that I couldn't imagine would help Mr. Marshall get back his good name.

At the same time—in December, I had been contacted by a couple of people who were interested in my manuscript for the purpose of making a movie. I didn't think much of it at first, but certainly wanted to pursue the possibility. They were thinking "made for TV" movie, and so many people had thought my story was perfect for that venue, I got quite interested in their proposal. I met with them several times and we were off to a good start when they then told me they were now pursuing a big-screen movie. Wow! Could this be?

The calls I would get were starting to sound amazing. Big-name scriptwriter. Big-name Director. I loved it, but, of course, I was very skeptical. There was no way I was going to get too excited until I signed a contract. The prior year I had a contract with a very well-respected book agent and I thought they'd be fighting over my book. Well, that didn't happen, I was told, because there was already a book in the works by Meryl Gordon that was to be published in November 2008. Would the public support yet another book on the subject? No one bit. But I was determined to get my book published one way or another, and even if there was a movie made, movies dramatize and take license. I wanted my book published as I wrote it with the truth set down for all to read. Even if I had to publish it myself. As it turned out, the movie deal never got off the ground so I'm glad I am a skeptic!

I had spoken to Linda Gillies late in March 2009, and she had told me she was scheduled to testify on April 21st, assuming all went as planned. But from what I read in *The New York Times*, both sides were being very careful about jury selection, and that could delay the start of the trial. I'd also heard from Meryl Gordon, the author of *Mrs. Astor Regrets*, who was covering the trial for *Vanity Fair* Magazine, that much of the jury selection was being done in private because so much personal information was being asked of the jurors. She'd heard that once a jury was seated, there would be a week's break before the actual trial started. Sure enough, Linda Gillies, who would be the first to testify, e-mailed me on April 17th that the jury had been selected and she would be called on April 28th. It was showtime.

By coincidence, I received a jury duty notice to start serving on April 27th. At first I thought I would ask for a postponement, but when I called the court and explained I had to be available to testify, the clerk said I could still serve my jury duty and if need be I would be allowed to be absent when I was needed at the trial.

All my family and friends wanted to be present when I testified, but I was sure the courtroom wouldn't hold all my supporters. I did want a few people there—like my husband, my sister and at least one friend. I was not nervous about testifying, but I did not look forward to seeing the Marshalls. I just had a feeling I would not react well to being in their presence. It would bring back so many memories—both good and bad—of our past. So I would be happy to have a few faces in front of me that were comforting.

I was also thinking how I wished I could tell my parents, both of whom were long gone, that I finally felt that my college education in sociology and psychology had paid off! I'd spent quite a bit of time during the years I worked for Mrs. Astor analyzing what made Brooke Astor and Anthony Marshall tick. I'd seen a mother/son relationship that was so foreign to what I experienced among people I was close to. Again, I'm sure they loved each other as mother and son, but the more I witnessed between them, the more I felt they did not *like* each other and that there were too many unspoken feelings between them. Certainly, when Mrs. Astor's health was getting worse, her son did not come across as mourning her decline. What I did not like was that Mrs. Astor had been warehoused before she died, and her legacy had been changed mostly for Charlene's benefit. That seemed the opposite of everything Mrs. Astor had planned. I kept thinking: *Does it make sense that a woman would wait until she was 101 years old to make changes to her will?* Common sense said to me that certainly by age 100 you would make sure all your papers were in order in case you didn't wake up the next morning!

Back to the trial. It began on April 27th, the same day as my jury service began. I was concerned about bumping into the Marshalls when I found out the trial was right down the hall from the jury assembly room. But I was dismissed from jury duty after speaking to the clerk and telling him I was going to testify at the Astor trial. I did not want any conflicts to arise. The clerk made a call and then excused me, telling me I was scheduled to testify the following week. That was news to me. I had spoken with the DA's office the prior Friday, and they did not have me scheduled yet. But I wasn't going to argue.

Linda Gillies was the first person called to testify. I asked her to call me afterwards and let me know what it had been like. This was a new experience for most of us. Every day, I would check the newspapers to see who testified. If you are testifying, you are not allowed to go into the courtroom and watch the proceedings, so I never got to hear any of the other witnesses. I sure would have liked to see and hear the action rather than just read relay on what the newspapers reported.

So I read of the many friends and associates of Mrs. Astor who testified: Betsy Gotbaum, Nancy Kissinger, Louis Auchincloss, Philippe de Montebello, Annette de la Renta, Lord Astor, several of her doctors, and on and on. I received a call to come in for another talk with the prosecutor during the second week of the trial—meaning that I would be up to testify soon—but the meeting was cancelled because things were moving slower than expected. I jotted down items reported in the newspaper that the witnesses spoke about that I felt should have been expanded on. (I didn't know if the newspapers simply hadn't reported enough about these issues or if the topic hadn't been gone into.)

For instance, the newspapers reported that Phillipe de Montebello said Mrs. Astor had offered to pay for the Buddha, but after Mr. Marshall refused to honor her offer—saying that she couldn't afford it--the museum ended up taking the money from a fund Mrs. Astor had previously given them. (I had been originally told by Chris Ely that Annette de la Renta had offered to pay for the Buddha in Mrs. Astor's name, but that evidently was not what happened.)

But I couldn't help speculating that if Mrs. Astor didn't have the money for the Buddha, or if she was in no mental condition to offer the money, then certainly the same would go for the $250,000 check from Mrs. Astor that Mr. Marshall had me write and send to Barking Dog Productions just a few weeks later for use in a future theater production. And when the sale of the painting by Childe Hassam came up in court, I wondered whether anyone had asked why Mrs. Astor would sell the painting at that point? She didn't need the cash. It would only increase in value if held. I believed that Mr. Marshall had encouraged her to sell the painting because he wanted the commission to buy the house in New Jersey.

Then there was that awful picture in the *New York Post* of Charlene crying. I really felt bad for her when I saw that. But once again I thought, *Why did you stop talking to me? What made you so much more aggressive when Mrs. Astor's health diminished?* As I reread the notes I kept, I was reminded that I had observed a drastic change in Charlene's attitude and demeanor, and lost my sympathetic feelings. This was a woman very involved in her church, St. James' on Madison Avenue and 71st Street. She was a mother of three who was very tight with her children. I had trouble understanding the Charlene I knew for the first nine years of our acquaintance with the Charlene I observed during the last three years I was still employed by Mrs. Astor.

Well, Charlene wasn't indicted for anything. But I couldn't help picturing in my mind, Charlene, Mr. Marshall and

Francis Morrissey sitting around the Marshall's apartment cooking up this scheme. From firing Terry Christensen to writing the codicils; from staging Mrs. Astor's reading of the proclamation at the Knickerbocker Club lunch to starting the Anthony D. Marshall Foundation; from becoming the co-executors of Mrs. Astor's will, to starting Delphi Productions; it appeared to me that these three formed a triumvirate that would pay off very well for all of them--as long as no one challenged what they were doing. And none of them could have imagined such a challenge.

But there we were.

The week of May 11th saw several of Mrs. Astor's past social secretaries testifying. Jolee Hirsch Fennebresque worked for Mrs. Astor for four years from 1997 to 2001. She left to work at the Bush White House. She is a lovely young lady who did a very admirable job as social secretary. After she left Mrs. Astor's employment, there were a string of social secretaries but no one lasted very long. Birgit Darby, the third try after Jolee, worked for a few months at the end of 2001, early 2002. Birgit testified about a phone conversation she'd had with Charlene Marshall during which Charlene was swearing and said, "If he dies, I get nothing," referring to Mr. Marshall. Naomi Packard Dunn-Koot was hired after Birgit was dismissed, and she stayed a year. The Marshalls hired Naomi and were very taken with her at first, but like all those who got close to Mrs.

Astor and watched over her, she fell out of favor and was on her way. Naomi came to New York to testify from her home in The Netherlands, where she was living with her husband and baby. After Naomi was let go, Erica Meyer, the friend of Mrs. Marshall's daughter, was hired. She testified after me in August, and from what I read in the *New York Daily News*, she said she did not believe Mrs. Astor understood what she was signing when she signed the codicils that Erica witnessed. I did not read anything about the fact that though Erica was hired as Mrs. Astor's social secretary, she worked mostly for Delphi and the Marshalls.

As I've written this story, I've slowly deduced that the Marshalls entry into the theatre world must have had a great deal to do with their change of attitude to everything. Suddenly they were giddy over their show business life and saw themselves as winners. Nothing was going to stop them from enjoying this euphoria—so they needed money to continue that life. They may have felt they had to secure as much of Mrs. Astor's money as possible—to be sure they were well entrenched in this new world of theirs. I'm more convinced now than ever that that was primary in their minds. Francis Morrissey was also involved in Delphi, so it all makes sense.

For seven days, Henry Christensen, the lawyer, was on the stand. In my opinion, he was key in finding out just what had gone on between Mr. Marshall and Mrs. Astor and the wills. How I wished I could have been in the court to hear his testimony. All I could do was read about it like everyone else--but I was frustrated by the lack of in depth reporting. *The New York Post*, on May 29, 2009, reported that Mr. Christensen said that Mrs. Astor wished to make her son happy "but she didn't want to see money go to Charlene." Mr. Christensen was serving both Mrs. Astor and the Marshalls. And that could not have been easy.

The parade of witnesses went on and I was most interested in knowing what my fellow long term ex-employees were saying in court. Mily de Gernier, Mrs. Astor's housekeeper, who one newspaper said was French and spoke with a thick French accent, is Swiss and speaks with a German accent! So I'm not sure whether to believe what was written about her testimony! Chris Ely, the butler, was on the stand on June 9. He was very close to Mrs. Astor for eight years before he was fired, and attended to her every whim.

Marciano Amaral, the chauffeur, testified on Tuesday, June 23. Given what I read in the papers, he must have done a great job. He did not let them confuse him, and said some bold things. Marciano had spent a great deal of time with Mrs. Astor alone; he not only listened to her vent, he also heard conversations between her and others in the back seat of the car. The defense tried to paint him as angry at Mr. Marshall for firing him, but Marciano went on to a better

job, so in the end he was quite pleased with where he'd landed. Marciano would have stayed with Mrs. Astor until the
end as he promised her, if he'd been allowed.

I had my next meeting with Joel Seidemann on Friday, June
12, for three hours. We went over what questions he would
ask me. And he noted that the defense attorneys would probably try to "get" me on my book, saying that that's what I
would be promoting. Well, I started keeping notes back in
2003 because I was very disturbed with the bad behavior I
was witnessing. At that time, I had no intention of writing a
book—only, perhaps, an article after Mrs. Astor died about
my experience with her. *She* was the interesting subject, not
Mr. and Mrs. Marshall.

But as time went by and I kept more notes and copies of
questionable bills, I collected a treasure trove of information
that certainly would contribute to a good book. So, yes, I
intended to publish the truth about what I saw. The whole
truth. I was advised by Joel that there were several things I
couldn't say in court—and this baffled me. He said the judge
had ruled that certain information could not be addressed.
Hmmmm...is this justice? I thought I would have to swear
to tell the truth, the whole truth, and nothing but the truth.
So why would I be told I then couldn't say that Mrs. Astor
said to me "Tony says I'm spending too much money. Am I
spending too much money?" Or, I could not mention that
one of Mr. Marshall's present lawyers, Kenneth Warner, was

one of the attorneys hired after Mr. Christensen was fired in 2004 to be the litigator who eventually got Mr. Christensen to turn over the wills and codicil to the new attorneys for Mrs. Astor—Morrissey and Whitaker.

Then Warren Whitaker was on the stand. He was the attorney who had Mrs. Astor sign the second codicil. He did not meet Mrs. Astor before the signing that day, so how could he know what her condition was? He states, according to the newspaper report, that she was competent on that day at that time. It's mind boggling that she was always competent on the days she signed codicils, but otherwise was slipping. Three codicils, three sharp moments in an otherwise mentally confused state. That is confusing!

Mr. Whitaker is a very well-regarded estates attorney so I could not fathom how or why he got involved in all of this. Was it the Astor name?

Anyway, June 22, 2009 I was riding back from Indiana, where my husband and I had spent the weekend. I got a call from my dear friend Linda with a small-world story.
A friend of hers was a real estate agent and recently showed a house selling for between $3 and 4 million to none other than Charlene's daughter Inness and her husband. Now where on earth would Inness get that kind of money? Let's see......If you guessed that my very first thought was that Charlene would be coming up with the funds, you would be

correct. I told Philip when we first spoke that Mrs. Astor's legacy was being changed, and this was an example of what I meant. Not only might Tony take care of Charlene, but, of course, her three offspring.

Finally, Lourdes Hilario, my office colleague and dear friend, testified on July 2nd. She had been so nervous that I thought she'd pass out when her day came! But she pulled through swimmingly and just answered the questions to the best of her knowledge. She had called me about four times that morning for a pep talk! And afterward, she prepped me by telling me to listen very carefully to the questions and make sure you understand them before you reply.

The parade continued. Pearline Noble and Minnette Christie, Mrs. Astor's nurses. Pearline, the day nurse, was on the stand for five days giving minute details from her notes. And I loved the story of Mrs. Astor's maid, Angela Moore, who testified that she saw Charlene walk over to Mrs. Astor in the hospital room when she broke her hip and tell her she ruined their vacation—they had to cancel their trip to London. The defense hinted that Angela either had heard wrong or perhaps Charlene had been joking. But Angela was not persuaded. She stuck to her testimony like glue.

Finally, it was my turn. I met with Joel Seidemann again on July 24th from 11:30 -5:30, to review questions, and I testified on July 27th. Every time I did a review something new came to light. Joel and I were talking about Mr. Marshall's pledge to the Marine Corps University Fund of $1million. I wrote the check from Mrs. Astor's account for the first installment of $270,000. This was to endow a fund of some sort in Mr. Marshall's name. It struck me that later that year, 2005, Mr. Marshall told me that he was finally being honored at the annual Marine Corps luncheon, in November, given in his grandfather's name, John Russell. And Mr. Marshall had indicated to me that it was "about time." I now see that there must have been a connection. Wake up, Alice!

I thought about what to wear to court. All my female friends and relatives asked me what I'd be wearing! I originally thought that my court date would be in the winter. I had a suit picked out—a very businesslike look. Then the trial was moved to spring. I came up with a new outfit, for a warmer day. Now it was the middle of summer and just too hot for the suit look. So I chose a black straight silk skirt and turquoise top that buttons down the front, black heels and pearl accessories. Simple. Ladylike. Not too austere, but not casual. I felt comfortable. And Lourdes and I had agreed that we should wear to court what we would have worn to the office. We always wore skirts, never pants, to work; it was just an unspoken rule.

I was not really nervous. But testifying was something so totally out of the ordinary—something I'd never done before—that I was certainly tense. I know that all I had to do was listen to the question, be sure I understood it, and tell the truth. What could be more straightforward? Well, I heard that the defense attorneys may try to trick you into saying something you might not mean. So you must be sure that you understand what they are looking for. I hoped that my mind was sharp enough, and was determined to get a good night's sleep.

My alarm went off at 6 a.m. July 27th after a night of surface sleep. I got ready and headed out to take the subway downtown. I was due at Joel's office at 8 a.m., so I picked up some coffee and arrived a little early. We again quickly reviewed materials, and then we were off to the courtroom. My husband, Joe, was waiting for me and we were ushered into the witness room where I remained until called—a very stark room with a table and a few chairs and three windows facing south. That's it. Joe left me and went into the courtroom to watch from the beginning.

Of all the people who thought they might come to see me, only my cousins Ellen and Al Rosenblatt showed up. In the middle of summer, everyone was somewhere else. There were press there and a few onlookers, but otherwise it was not very crowded. As I was called into the court, I quickly walked across the room to the witness chair beside the judge. Once I was seated and I put on my glasses, I took a good sweeping look around the room and deliberately stared at each person. The judge, the defense lawyers, Mr. Morrissey, Mr.

Marshall, Charlene, the prosecutors and the jury. I wanted to be comfortable in knowing who was there and where each was located. I was not nervous for some very strange reason, but I was wound up. I knew I had to keep my head clear and concentrate.

I was amazed at how much the prosecutor was not allowed to ask me, and more amazed at what the defense did not ask me. I was told later that this lack of questioning by the defense was to keep from opening up topics the defense did not want to address. So several of the questions I'd gone over many times with the prosecutor were not brought up. The defense seemed to want to get across that Mr. Marshall was thrifty because he was a child of the depression!! Wow. I didn't recall ever hearing or reading anything about his life being affected at all by the depression. Mrs. Astor never lived in poverty, no matter which husband she was married to. In fact, I recall Mr. Marshall's telling me that he was hiking in Switzerland with his mother and stepfather when they learned that Germany had invaded Poland. Wasn't that during the depression?

Then, near the end of my testimony, which took all day from around 10:15 a.m. to 5:30 p.m., the defense put in front of me annual-income statements for Mrs. Astor for the years 1998 through 2005 and asked me, "Mrs. Perdue, isn't it true....Mrs. Astor spent more money than she received every year except for 2002 based on this document?"

Every year showed a loss except for the year 2002 when Mr. Marshall sold the Childe Hassam painting. Well, I took one look and said, "I would question the validity" of the document. Because Lourdes and I worked in tandem in the office, I was always aware what was happening financially. She kept the records of investments and banking, but everything passed over my desk. When she and I were losing money hand over fist in our personal accounts, we were impressed how Mrs. Astor almost always made money due to the high end investors who handled her money. Option traders. Hedge funds.

Specifically, Lourdes had told me at the end of 2001, Mrs. Astor made so much money in 2001 that we were going to have huge taxes to pay. She suggested to the accountant that perhaps it was a good time to ask Mr. Marshall if he'd consider setting up a retirement fund for us which would come out of office expense. Well, it turns out that the accountant did mention this to Mr. Marshall, and the result was that Mr. Marshall gave himself a check for $50,000 and charged it to office expenses. But we did not get a retirement fund. In subsequent years he'd add a big bonus for himself. And he took a $5 million gift in 2003. *That's* how you would see a negative earnings statement. It had been positive until extra money was drawn by Mr. Marshall *for* Mr. Marshall. I further found out that none of the statements included the hedge funds. But the defense attorney wanted the jury to believe that Mr. Marshall sold the Hassam painting to make money for Mrs. Astor and that was the only year she had a positive earnings statement. How absurd!

Several times during the testimony, both the jury and I had to leave the room so the lawyers could have a powwow with the judge. Later, my husband told me he could hear a little of what was going on, and they were arguing about what could be admitted. But in the end, Joel Seidemann, the prosecutor who questioned me, got his points across because the defense, by showing the earnings statements, opened up the ability for Joel to show checks I wrote for Mr. Marshall's benefit that reduced Mrs. Astor's income.

One of the reporters was from the *New York Post*, and my cousin Ellen overheard him say I did not look 62. So I really like him! But a headline in the *New York Post* article the next day was "Charlene Rips That Bitch" and I am presumably the bitch. I guess I should wear that as a badge of honor. All I did was tell the truth, and that's what one has to do in court. *The New York Times* and the *New York Daily News* also wrote articles.

Looking at Mr. Marshall in the courtroom, I really still felt some sympathy though I did know what he had done. I thought it was sad that this was how he was spending his old age. And Charlene—well, I just didn't get her at all. But I couldn't help but wonder how a lay minister could behave and speak the way she did. And I wondered what her family and friends thought of her behavior. Were they impressed? Did they get it?

When the trial was over, I thought the proceedings had shown how money can cause normal people to do nasty things. Though I was pretty sure the jury had to believe after all the testimony that Mrs. Astor was in no position to be changing her will and benefiting her daughter-in-law that late in the game, I figured it was possible they would have found Mr. Marshall "not guilty" just based on his age and service to his country. That seemed a possibility. And I didn't want to see him go to jail. Maybe house arrest. But the money needed to go where Mrs. Astor had intended it to go. And I imagined Charlene would still end up financially comfortable whatever the verdict.

My prospective book was not brought up in court, nor the fact that I had kept notes for so long. So much of what I thought I'd get a chance to say in court was disallowed. This was precisely why a book by me was imperative—I wanted down on paper everything I witnessed as a catharsis for me and a record for all. My hope is that this book not only honors Mrs. Astor, but warns the public about financial elder abuse. We all need to be more precise about how our meager or grand estate is handled after our death.

The good thing about this very long trial is that it brought to the forefront the problem of financial elder abuse. We know it is pervasive, but it is one of those family secrets that rarely gets out—unless it is a sensational story. I've read that those in the legal profession involved in elder abuse watched this case very closely and will undoubtedly use it as a precedent in future arguments. With the Baby Boom generation reaching old age, it is certainly time for a more exact way to nail down one's final desires when it comes to financials. The tougher part is the actual physical care. Empathy and kindness cannot be ordered by the courts. It's still pretty much luck what happens to each of us in the end.

We've all heard stories about people duping a parent into signing something when the parent was no longer understanding what he was signing. I'd heard children argue and become estranged siblings because of what one or the other did. It's a fact of life. If someone has money and is dying, someone wants that money, whether it be $50,000 or $50,000,000.

It is obvious that some plan is needed for an older person to have a nonpartisan person in attendance when legal documents are signed. Not the person's lawyer, doctor or family member, but someone without any connection to the signer. There could be a list of questions the signer must answer in private with the nonpartisan person to prove that the document is understood and being signed of one's own free will.

I don't suppose it is possible to think of every situation that could arise when one grows old, and there is probably no way to make provisions that will cover all the *ifs* and *buts*. However, it would be comforting to know that if someone makes out a will, it could not be changed without very scrupulous steps taken to ensure the signer was *compos mentis*.

On many days during the last two and a half years that I worked for Mrs. Astor, Lourdes and I would leave the office together at the end of the workday and stand outside the office building reviewing what transpired that day. We'd jokingly say, "We are going to end up on *Larry King Live*!" It all seemed so surreal to us. The building manager would come out and say, "Don't you two see enough of each other all day? Go home!" We could go on and on theorizing why Mr. Marshall did what he did, and we continue to talk about it to this day. But I'm ready to let it go, as soon as this book is published. I will have said my piece, and I can rest my case.

CHAPTER ELEVEN

THE VERDICT

I was on the telephone with a reporter from the *New York Post*—Stefanie Cohen—when she suddenly announced to me, "There's a verdict!" It was Thursday, October 8, 2009, and the jury had been out for 12 days. I had been concerned that there might be a mistrial due to a report of a juror's feeling threatened. Having served on several juries myself, I knew how emotions can erupt.

But there it was. Mr. Marshall was convicted on 14 of the 16 counts against him. On the one hand, I felt sad for him; on the other hand, I felt vindicated. What I had seen happening before my eyes for more than two years, others had confirmed was, in fact, criminal.

I was perplexed by the defense—or rather, lack of defense. Mr. Marshall's lawyers called no witnesses. At the very least, I thought that Mr. Marshall, if he believed in his own innocence, would have defended himself. Couldn't he have raised some doubt in the minds of the jurors? Or did he realize as the trial went on and on that he indeed had behaved badly? He could not possibly have thought, given all those witnesses the prosecution presented, that he was not going to be convicted.

I had no doubt that Morrissey would be found guilty of forgery. Just look at those signatures on the three codicils! In my opinion, by March 2004, when the third one was signed, Mrs. Astor could never have written her name as strongly as it appeared on the document. Morrissey was convicted of five of the six charges against him in the indictment, including the forgery of the signature.

The sentencing was set for December 2009. Mr. Marshall received a sentence of one to three years in prison on a first–degree grand larceny charge (giving himself $1 million for managing his mother's estate) and concurrent one-year sentences on the other 13 counts. Morrissey received concurrent one to three year sentences for his convictions for scheming to defraud and grand larceny. The two defendants were free while their cases were appealed.

The *New York Post* asked me to write a piece under my by-line—they wanted an insider's story. So I obliged and gave a little glimpse into what I was writing in this book. The article appeared in the Sunday, October 11, 2009 edition.

Since then there have been many articles and blogs ranging from social comments on how upset Mrs. Astor would be to have this mess revealed publicly to the changes that the trial will trigger regarding estate planning and competency. It is my hope that the good results of the trial will outweigh the tacky details that emerged from a thorough investigation into just what happened to Mrs. Astor.

June of 2003 has always been the dividing line for me. That day, the day Mrs. Astor broke her hip for the second time, was the day that made all the difference in the lives of many. As I wrote in the *New York Post* article, the juxtaposition of the Marshalls' new theater life and Mrs. Astor's rapid decline set the stage for an aggressive plan to secure as much of Mrs. Astor's fortune as possible before her demise. The Marshalls were riding high and reaping the accolades of many in the theatre world, and I believe that they wanted to be sure that exciting life continued. To do that, they needed as much capital as possible to invest in stage productions—a risky business. And Mrs. Astor had all that "capital" just sitting there waiting to go to charities—why not to the Marshalls?

My final thought about Mrs. Astor is that I feel privileged to have known her. She wasn't perfect and I know she could be difficult. But I was lucky to have had a very congenial and positive relationship with her. Whenever I was in her company, I could feel the spark she emitted that drew people to her. I guess that's what is called charisma. She had it to the nth degree and it served her and the city of New York very well.

EPILOGUE

In March of 2012, the Surrogate Court in Westchester County settled Mrs. Astor's estate. The Court was going to wait until Mr. Marshall's appeal was decided, but that would go on for some time. The Court upheld the 2002 will but threw out the three codicils to that will. The New York State Attorney General's office negotiated the settlement, and I, personally, was satisfied with the results.

However, I was disappointed to hear that my friend Lourdes, who has now retired to California, only got $1000 per year of service as her severance package. She certainly deserved the same package I got when I was dismissed. Nothing changed in that arena.

Mrs. Astor's jewelry, art and household furnishings were auctioned off at Sotheby's in New York on September 24 and 25, 2012. I attended the auction for a few hours each day, and it was fascinating to watch. Many items sold for way beyond the estimates assigned to them. And, of course, some things sold below estimate. However, in the end, Sotheby's took in almost $19 million, quite a bit above the $6-9 million estimated.

I was amazed that Mrs. Astor's emerald engagement ring from Vincent fetched $1 million after two bidders drove the price up, one on the phone and one in the room. The bidder in the room got it. Yet her prized possession--the emerald and diamond Bulgari necklace-- "only" brought in $570,000. The matching earrings brought another $125,000. And the over 10-carat double diamond ring that Mrs. Astor had given to Charlene (but Charlene had had to return) sold for $510,000. So I guess Mily and I truly were toting around millions of dollars worth of jewelry in our shopping bags! The good news is that all the money from the auction is going to charity. I should point out that Sotheby's adds on their percentage to the accepted bid that the buyer is responsible for paying. Thus, the final cost is quite a bit higher than what is bid.

Before the auction, I had been sent a gift from the estate from Philip and Alec Marshall of a Chinese export porcelain teapot as a memento of Mrs. Astor. It's lovely and fitting for me—since I am a heavy-duty tea drinker. However, I suspect I will put this teapot on display rather than use it. And I heard that Lourdes got a silver picture frame.

I saw Philip Marshall on the first day of the auction and got a very brief chance to say hello. But we caught up later by e-mail and he was delighted with the results of the auction.

It was sad to see all of Mrs. Astor's belongings being dispersed but it was also a reminder of the incredible life she lived--and did so to the fullest. There was a young woman sitting in front of me at the auction on the second day who bid on, and got, two items. It turned out that her husband had been on the jury that convicted Mr. Marshall, and they wanted some meaningful mementos of the many months of their lives that had been interrupted.

I hope all of us who now own a piece of Mrs. Astor's life enjoy the items but also remember that this was a woman who not only lived a life of luxury, but devoted time, energy and money to bettering the lives of other people. Something we all should do.

Finally, on March 26, 2013, a New York State appellate court upheld the convictions of both Anthony Marshall and Frances X. Morrissey, Jr. Mr. Morrissey was taken into custody on June 20th, and Mr. Marshall followed on June 21st.

I again felt sad to think of my former boss going to prison, especially at his advanced age of 89 and with many health issues. I thought that house arrest would make more sense. He was obviously not a "danger" to anyone, and why should the taxpayers foot the bill for his needed care? Well, after just two months of incarceration, Mr. Marshall was granted medical parole and left the system on August 22nd. And so the story ends.

Mrs. Astor's 95th birthday, March 1997

ACKNOWLEDGMENTS

I thank my husband Joe Perdue, my sister Susan and brother-in-law Bernard Cooper, who has since passed away, and my dear friends Linda and Don Sage for encouraging me to write this book and then keeping at me until it was in print. Many people read the manuscript and made comments or suggestions for which I am deeply grateful. For fear of leaving anyone out, I will not name them—they know who they are.

All my friends and family, and even strangers who I got into conversations with about Mrs. Astor, have been waiting patiently for the published manuscript. Well here it is, at last!

ABOUT THE AUTHOR

Alice Macycove Perdue is a native of Boston and a graduate of the University of Massachussetts, Amherst. She moved to New York City immediately after college and worked on the marketing and promotional side of the publishing business with Ziff-Davis, CBS and Readers Digest special interest magazines including *Psychology Today, Boating, Yachting, Car & Driver, Skiing, Modern Bride,* and *Travel Holiday.* She went to work for Brooke Astor in 1993. She and her husband, Joe, live in Manhattan and on Cape Cod.

Her collaborator on this book, James Seymore, had a long and distinguished career in journalism. He is a graduate of Princeton University. His first position was as a general assignment reporter for the *Richmond Times Dispatch.* He wrote for a number of publications before moving to Time Warner in New York where he would eventually become Executive Editor of *People* magazine and then Managing Editor of *Entertainment Weekly.* He and his wife, Joyce, live in Connecticut.

CPSIA information can be obtained at www.ICGtesting.com
Printed in the USA
LVOW07s0431220615

443343LV00001B/25/P